Konrad

Ku

mmel, Mary Richards Gray

In the Turkish camp

and other stories

Konrad
Ku
..
mmel, Mary Richards Gray

In the Turkish camp
and other stories

ISBN/EAN: 9783741112638

Manufactured in Europe, USA, Canada, Australia, Japa

Cover: Foto ©Andreas Hilbeck / pixelio.de

Manufactured and distributed by brebook publishing software (www.brebook.com)

Konrad Kummel, Mary Richards Gray

In the Turkish camp

In the Turkish Camp

AND

Other Stories.

From the German of Konrad Kuemmel.

BY

MARY RICHARDS GRAY.

ST. LOUIS, MO., 1899.
Published by B. HERDER,
17 South Broadway.

O the memory of my mother, the translator's share of this little book is dedicated.

CONTENTS.

		Page.
I.	In the Turkish Camp	7
II.	The Skull of Kara Mustapha	15
III.	The Star of Fortune	25
VI.	The Bells of Weyher	34
V.	The Saving of St. Damian's	40
VI.	Setis	44
VII.	The Mysterious Voice	52
VIII.	The Saying of the Oracle	58
IX.	The Vestal Virgins	68
X.	The Kiss of the Christ Child	73
XI.	The Artist of the Bregenz Wood	78
XII.	The Meeting	86
XIII.	A Cheering Word	94
XIV.	The Christ Child's Singer	102
XV.	Saint Augustine's Convert	109
XVI.	Christmas in the Snow	117
XVII.	Three Prayers	122
XVIII.	Ecce Homo	130

IN THE TURKISH CAMP.

IT was Advent in the year 1682. Daily there came disheartening news from the Turkish leader whose Mohammedan hordes threatened to overrun Europe.

At Vienna all was commotion. Envoys had come from the Hungarian rebel, Count Tököly, and, to the astonishment of the populace, they were admitted to the very presence of the Emperor himself, and were allowed to wear their swords, a privilege accorded only to faithful knights. The mien of these men was neither conciliatory nor humble, yet the Emperor hoped for the best. Knowing the indifference of his own German princes, men absorbed in the affairs of their kingdoms, he wished to win to his side, and to the cause of Christianity, these Hungarian magnates; so he treated the envoys with distinction and sent them away from the palace, loaded with gifts.

Little heeding the shouts of the people they rode down the street, and upon arriving at their lodging place entered and retired to a closed chamber for conference.

"The Emperor dreams a dream!" cried one scornfully.

"He fancies we have come on his account. Ah, if his Majesty up there in the royal palace only knew all! While we were exchanging fine compliments, our Aschmed Bey was making plans for the destruction of the royal city. And when those are ready, then, farewell Emperor! We will take the plans to our master, and he will give them to the Sultan, who will move directly on Vienna, conquer it, and reward his servants royally. Aschmed Bey, will you not be ready soon?"

In the adjoining room sat a man of thirty marking industriously on a map of Vienna. His pale face was framed in dark hair and beard; his eyes had a hunted look in their depths, his glance wandered about restlessly, and now and then a shadow passed over his brow as of some dark remembrance flitting through his mind.

"How much longer must we wait?" asked one of the messengers gruffly.

"Eight days more, your lordship," was the answer, "so that I may spend each night, as I have already done, in going about undisturbed and seeing all the city."

In the Turkish Camp.

"O hasten, Aschmed! If our errand be known, speedy and direful will be our fate," so spoke Count Tököly's ambassadors, traitors to their Emperor, worthy representatives of him who sent them, common spies in the service of the Turks.

The night was fast waning and the morning was breaking over Burg-Ravelin.* Stealthily a man stole along the castellated wall, scrutinizing with the eyes of a cat, as if he would impress upon his memory every corner, every nook, every inch of ground.

Finally the man arose as if content. A sound broke the stillness of the air, the morning Angelus calling the faithful to prayer. Instinctively the spy raised his hand to his forehead to bless himself, then let it fall to his side.

Silent, stupified, he stood like one within whose mind some great struggle was going on, as in the morning twilight the bells pealed forth with a deep, clear tone like the warning call of conscience.

This bell, heard again after so many years, brought to him a strange message, a premonition of evil.

"Ave Maria," came faintly from his lips,

---
* Burg-Ravelin is the chief fortress of Vienna.

and he lifted his hat and stood for an instant with bowed head. Then Aschmed Bey went down from Burg-Ravelin and through the streets of the city, in which flickered here and there the light of lanterns.

Silent figures passed him, wrapped in long fur mantles, all going toward the church from which a faint light glimmered. Involuntarily Aschmed Bey, the spy, followed the churchgoers.

"It is the early mass," he said to himself, "and Advent season," and entering the church, he knelt unnoticed near the door and buried his face in his hands.

A tiny bell rang, the priest came from the sacristy, the organ pealed forth solemnly, and mass was celebrated before the people with the utmost devotion.

Only one in all the audience felt ill at ease, the Turkish spy, Aschmed Bey, kneeling on the farthermost bench. And yet he belonged here for his deportment, his posture, the tears that trickled through the fingers with which he covered his face, bespoke Christian training.

His past rose before him and he saw standing on a lonely mountain, a monastery with red roof and tiny turrets and close beside it a poor little church, on the plastered walls of which were the Stations of the Cross.

In the peaceful seclusion, round about the church, bloomed many beautiful wild flowers and here the monks wandered, upon their faces an expression of peace, the peace which the world can not give.

He saw one of them, young, happy and enthusiastic in the quiet life of the monastery until temptation came, and the Christian monk foreswore country and religion and became Aschmed Bey, the Turk.

Honor, applause, and gold were his reward. Donning the Turkish costume, as an engineer and one skilled in military tactics, he went from place to place, throughout Christendom.

With the messengers sent out by Count Tököly, he had spied about the fortifications of the old capital in the very heart of Austria, that he might betray the weak places to the enemy and then himself conduct the siege.

Such had been the life of Aschmed Bey, monk, traitor, spy!

Of the worshippers about him none knew what went on in the heart of the spy. Silent, sad and earnest, he rose and passed out of the church, alone as he had come.

Some months later Aschmed Bey stood before the Sultan and gave to him and Kara Mustapha the plans of the city of Vienna. The Unbelievers received the priceless treasures with great joy and said:

"Thou hast performed a great service for Allah and his Prophet. Ask one favor and it shall be granted thee."

Aschmed's eyes sparkled and in a clear, ringing voice he said:

"O Sultan, make me master of the guns and director of the mines to be built under the walls of Vienna. I know well where the weakest places are in the fortifications."

"Thy request is granted," replied the Sultan, and Aschmed Bey, the former Capuchin monk, became head engineer at the siege of Vienna.

On July 14, 1683, the city was surrounded. For two days the cannon boomed incessantly, for two months the guns hurled against the unhappy city a half million bombs filled with combustibles, and numberless mines filled with explosives were placed under the walls and fortifications.

All was done under Aschmed Bey's watchful care and supervision. Whole nights he

In the Turkish Camp.

spent in the powder-magazines looking after the bombs, and his was the last hand to see that the fuses were ready.

But strange to say the fire-balls and bombs would not explode. Hundreds of them flamed up a little, then went out. Similar fire-balls reduced the city of Genoa to ashes in three days, but in Vienna during the fearful siege of two months, although quantities of fire and powder were hurled against it, scarcely two houses were burned. Of the twelve great mines filled with powder, seven exploded backward toward the Turkish camp, and instead of harming the besieged wrought havoc in the ranks of the besiegers.

Why this failure?

Aschmed Bey could have given information, could have told who spoiled the powder, and placed the mines so that instead of turning their deadly fire on the Christians, it was turned upon the Turks. Oft in his tent in the dead of night, tossing restlessly upon his divan, he murmured: "I, too, belong to those who guard against the Turks. Will God look kindly upon me if the city is saved? The prayer of the Christian world for the salvation of Vienna shall succeed through me."

September 12, 1683, Vienna was free. On every hand were loud rejoicings, save amongst the Turks, where gloom and rage possessed the heart of each warrior. Aschmed Bey's name was in every mouth, hatred of him in every breast, and fearing for his life, he fled to the distant fastnesses of the mountains.

* * *

In a wretched little house up in the Seven Mountains some years later, a priest sat at the bedside of a dying man and listened with streaming eyes to a confession. Then the priest administered the last rites and rose to go. Embracing the penitent he said: "Farewell, friend. You have sinned, you have atoned. You have repented. God knows the rest. I go to say a mass for your poor soul."

From the tiny church near by the music could be heard distinctly and the dying man deeply moved by it roused and cried, but in a scarce audible whisper:

"O Christ be merciful! Blessed Mary, pray for me!"—then sinking back upon the pillow, his soul took flight, the sinful, repentant soul of Aschmed Bey, once the foremost engineer in the Turkish camp.

The Skull of Kara Mustapha.

ALL Christendom was in direst woe. From one end of Europe to the other was heard the sound of Turkish bells, and the suppliant prayer of a million people crying:

"O Lord, save Thy people from the hands of their enemies!"

Kara Mustapha, the Grandvizier of the Sultan, had sworn on honor and life to place the Turkish crescent upon the walls of Vienna, and to obtain richest booty, and so he had laid siege to the royal city.

Proudly he stood at the door of his splendid tent, fitted up with costly rugs and luxurious appointments, and gazed at unhappy, besieged Vienna, which lay surrounded by a cloud of dust and smoke. Silently Kara Mustapha gazed. Near him was the messenger from the Turkish Sultan, who had brought to him, the commander-in-chief of the Turkish forces, a fine sword, a great gold medal and other costly presents, as a reward for his services.

"The Commander of the Faithful thanks you most heartily," said the messenger to

Kara Mustapha, "for always thinking of him so dutifully. The gold and silver treasures taken from churches and monasteries delighted him, but he is especially pleased with the great number of young Christian slaves, whom you have sent to him."

"Tell thy Lord and Master," was Mustapha's haughty reply, "that a much richer gift awaits him. Soon fifty thousand Christians will be on their way to Stamboul. You should have heard the weeping and wailing in the towns and villages through which we passed on our way here, when I ordered the old and the very young to be put to death, and selected those in the vigor of manhood and those in the bloom of youth to be kept for the Sultan and for myself, some to work on our intrenchments against their beloved Vienna, others for slaves in the royal palace.

"It was a splendid sight!* Three hundred thousand corpses mark my path from Belgrade

---

* Onno Klopp, the historian, says that in four small jurisdictions the following were killed by the Turks: 229 married people, 46 children and 89 servants. Those sent into slavery were: 215 married people, 518 children, 275 servants. Total 1372 persons murdered or reduced to slavery.

to Vienna and quite three hundred thousand Christian dogs are reduced to slavery. That is the anger of the Prophet and the work of my good right arm!"

Kara Mustapha closed his egotistic speech to the messengers from the Sultan with these words:

"And now Ali Aga, remain here five days; then you will be able to announce to my most honored Master, the Sultan, that Vienna has fallen, or in any case that its fall is near at hand.

"When Vienna's gates are ours, all Europe will be open to us. We will go through Germany by way of the Rhine; we will march through Italy and Spain and there our African brethren will greet us. The name of the hated Christian God shall be effaced from the whole world and from Stamboul to Gibraltar, Allah and his Prophet alone shall be worshipped.

"Say to the Sultan, our Master, that on the day when he called me to Belgrade to make me commander-in-chief of the Turkish forces, and handed over to me the great flag of the Prophet, I swore that the Christians should be driven out of Europe, the Christian God forgotten, and His churches turned into Mohammedan mosques. I will fulfil my vow; I, Kara Mustapha, the Grandvizier of the Sultan, will destroy the Kingdom of the Babe of Bethlehem!"

Ali Aga listened and waited, but instead of the triumph predicted, he saw Sobieski, King of Poland, with his followers rush down through the steep and dangerous mountain passes, and attack the Mohammedan forces that outnumbered his by thousands. All the carefully laid Turkish plans failed, and Kara Mustapha was ignominiously compelled to retreat.

Kara Mustapha was beside himself with rage over the issue.

"Oh master," said a spy to him, "there is one far more to blame for our defeat than Sobieski or Starhemberg, and that is Count Kollonitsch, the Bishop of Wiener-Neustadt. The Bishop holds the people together and is more dangerous to you than a whole army. He has a soldier's blood in his veins and has often smelled powder. Until he was thirty-five years of age he was a Knight of Malta, and he has already slain many Turks. He became a priest, then a bishop, and is now the Master of Vienna.

"When others were fleeing from the Capital, he entered it. He needs nothing for himself; his clothes are old and patched, and often for his midday meal he has only a piece of bread or an egg. By his example and courage he has inspired the most timid and cowardly. It is impossible to spread dissension in the ranks of the Viennese so long as he is there, for he keeps peace and unity among the people. He directs the nursing of the wounded and has untold sums of money with which he pays the soldiers and buys all necessary supplies. There is no end to his purse, and the Viennese cry: 'So long as Kollonitsch lives, Vienna cannot fall!'"

Kara Mustapha on hearing this, in anger drew his sword from its sheath and cried:

"Hear me, ye Ottomans, ye who are present here. So truly as Allah lives and Mohammed is his Prophet, so truly as I am a warrior of the Prophet, so surely will I, with this my good sword, cut off the head of that accursed bishop, and I command that not one of you touch a hair of his head. I can punish him!"*

So swore the Turk.

Kollonitsch, the Bishop, prayed during the

---

* This oath is quoted exactly.

hours left after his arduous daily tasks, and thousands joined with him morning, noon and night.

When the matin bells rang out and carried from mountain to mountain, from vale to vale, the great mystery and wonder, "The word became flesh and dwelt among us," united Christendom on bended knee, in churches, fields, streets and markets, with uplifted hands prayed for deliverance from the Turks.

That prayer was answered and the gentle Babe of Bethlehem showed to the barbarians, that He alone held the scepter of the world.

On the 12th of September of this same year, after the Turks had besieged Vienna for nine weeks, King Sobieski of Poland, the Prince of Lothringia, and Elector Max of Bavaria, with a small army coming down through the dangerous passes of the Kahlenberg mountains, attacked the Mohammedan horde unexpectedly and put them to route, saving Vienna.

Among the trophies that King Sobieski obtained was the flag which Kara Mustapha had received from the Sultan's own hand on the day of his departure from Belgrade.

With his whole army Kara Mustapha fled to Gran, thence to Pesth, and finally took

The Skull of Kara Mustapha.

refuge in Belgrade whence he had set out with so much pomp and splendor.

All these terrible defeats, however, did not soften his heart. Before leaving Vienna he caused the wholesale butchery of more than a thousand children and young persons, because he was unable to take them with him.

Kara Mustapha was cruel, but he was a Turk. A hundred times worse, more unpitying, more dishonorable, more base than he was Count Tököly, the leader of the Hungarians.

When the Count saw that things were going against the Turks, he played Kara Mustapha a cowardly trick. Presenting himself to the Sultan, with false representations he overthrew Kara Mustapha and ingratiated himself into the good-will of the Sultan. Count Tököly feared Kara Mustapha and took this way of overthrowing him.

On Christmas Day 1683 Kara Mustapha was notified that three deputies from the Sultan awaited him. He received them, Tschausch Baschi, Kapiglier Kiaja and the Captain of the Janissaries, and they stood silent in his presence, these messengers of death.

The Sultan had given audience to Count

Tököly and being convinced that Kara Mustapha was guilty of the defeats he had suffered, signed his death warrant.

These were the three commands of the Sultan.

The first: "Give up the great seal."
The Grandvizier obeyed.
The second: "Give up the flag."
He could not do this, as the flag was in possession of the Christians.

Then there was a pause, and finally Kara Mustapha broke the silence by saying: "Have you not another command for me?" He was pale as death, and cold perspiration stood on his brow. Was he thinking of the hundred thousand Christians whom he had dishonored, or had caused to be put mercilessly to death?

Silently the messenger handed him the paper. His death warrant was written upon it: "Kara Mustapha shall be strangled to death." After having been allowed a few moments for prayer, Kara Mustapha asked that his own slave might be allowed to strangle him, a request which was granted. In a few moments all was over and the head was taken to the Sultan, as a proof that his command had been obeyed.

The Skull of Kara Mustapha.

The mutilated body of Kara Mustapha was buried in Belgrade in a mosque which he had built with gold stolen from the Christians.

Five years after this when Bishop Kollonitsch had become Cardinal, he received a present, brought to him by two monks.

One of them said to the Cardinal: "Honored Master, as you well know, the Elector Max Emanuel, two months after the conquest of Belgrade, gave Mustapha's Mosque to our Order, that we might change it from a Turkish mosque into a Christian church, which has been done.

"Recently soldiers broke into the church, opened the grave in which lay the unrighteous Mohammedan and took out the treasures buried with him.

"We took from them this skull, this cord with which he was strangled and these sayings from the Koran, and knowing that every one in the Kingdom remembers Kara Mustapha's oath, and knowing, too, Most Honored Bishop, that he himself wished to cut off your head, we considered it best to bring to you these things, as a proof of the providence of God in watching over His church and His anointed."

Thereupon the speaker opened the chest

and showed the white skull of the fearful Kara Mustapha.

The Cardinal stood for a moment speechless, lost in meditation. He tried to picture to his mind the awful woe and suffering this head had planned and brought to Christendom. He saw the Grandvizier, honored and esteemed by his ruler, start out on his triumphal march from Belgrade to Vienna, and return to be foully murdered at the command of the master whom he had served so well.

Belgrade, the city that was the scene of his greatest triumph, was also the scene of his ignominious death.

"*Domine*," murmured the Cardinal, gazing fixedly at the skull of Kara Mustapha: "Thou hast put down the mighty from their seats and hath exalted them of low degree."

NOTE. The skull of Kara Mustapha may be seen to-day in the Armory in Vienna and the Turkish flag in the Holy House of Loretto, in Italy.

The Star of Fortune.

ON the morning of Ash Wednesday in the year 1810, Napoleon, the conqueror and master of Europe, was in his study in close conference with Marshal Berthier:

"On the fourth of March as Minister Extraordinary, you are to be my proxy at the Court of Vienna to celebrate my betrothal to the Archduchess Marie Louise, and on the eleventh the marriage by proxy is to take place there. I wish you, in my name to ask Archduke Charles of Austria, my opponent at Aspern, to be my proxy at the marriage. Then you are to bring my bride through the south of Germany to France. The Empress will receive a royal welcome at all the castles on the way, and at Branau, on the Bavarian frontier, my sister, the Queen of Naples, will meet her, and I myself will await her at Soissons. In the beginning of April our nuptials will be celebrated here in Paris. You are to attend to all matters of detail in furnishing and arranging our apartments, and as soon as all preparations for the journey are made, report to me."

The Marshal bowed low and left the room.

Napoleon was alone in his study. Slowly he rose and went to the high window, through which the bright winter sun sent in a flood of light and heat.

On his face there was an expression of unspeakable satisfaction.

"At last, — at last the goal is in sight!" he murmured, as through his mind there passed in quick review the events of his life of ambition, from the time he was a poor cadet until now Europe lay groveling at his feet. Since the time when scarcely twenty-seven years of age, he took chief command of the French army, his life had been a series of triumphs. His Empire stretched from the Pyrennees to the Baltic, and included Belgium, Holland, the Rhine country, the south of Germany, in fact, he held sway from the North Sea to Naples. Fifty million people were subject to him; and to princes born to the purple, he granted the privilege of holding their hereditary power but as vassals to him.

Great Austria lay powerless. A thousand tried army officers ably supported him and obeyed his every command. He overthrew every adversary. The treasures of all Europe were poured into France in accordance with his policy of enriching that country.

His power was absolute. Not a word of criticism was tolerated, not a newspaper in all the vast Empire dared do aught but flatter the Emperor.

At forty-one he was at the height of his success, and what he had won by his own will, his genius, he wished to hold and to hand down to posterity.

To bring about his heart's desire he was divorced from his wife, Josephine, by a prelate more devoted to him than to the Church. Then he, the son of an advocate, sought in marriage first the daughter of the royal house of Russia, and failing there, went to the Austrian Court, and obtained the promise of the hand of Marie Louise. The Austrian Emperor granted his request, not because he wished his daughter to marry him, but because he dared not refuse the demands of the world conqueror, as did the Russian Emperor. After robbing Francis II. of his power, and a part of the ancestral lands which he had inherited, he took his dearest treasure, his eldest daughter, the Archduchess Marie Louise, scarcely eighteen years of age, to dwell with him in Paris, hoping that God would bless their union with a family which would some day play the first role in the world.

In a few weeks the marriage celebrations would take place, and he wished them to be worthy of the greatest power in Europe. Twenty Cardinals were invited to Paris to assist at the nuptials and everything was to be on a grand scale.

Here Napoleon was aroused from his revery by the organ in the church near by and listening as the sounds died away he heard faintly the voice of the priests, saying: "Dust thou art, to dust thou shalt return."

* * *

A messenger had brought a letter that bore a Cardinal's seal. Napoleon tore it open and read it. His eyes flashed; with a set expression on his face he threw the letter on the floor and said:

"Thirteen Cardinals dare refuse to be present at my wedding. They do not object to my divorce, since they know my marriage was not a religious one, there being no witnesses present, yet they refuse to sanction a second one. They say my divorce was granted by a prelate who had no right to grant it. Enough! They shall not remain in Paris. They shall learn that I am master here. In my own dominions I am absolute sovereign. From this time forth, under penalty of death, I forbid those Cardinals wearing their scarlet robes.

"I degrade them to the rank of ordinary priests and I will assign to each a place in which to await my pleasure."

These orders were carried out, and a few days after this the thirteen Cardinals disappeared, going into small obscure towns.

"How long, O Lord, how long?" sighed one, an old gray-haired man, on parting with his friends.

"Is not the measure full enough yet?" complained a second. "Has this man not sinned enough against God and His Church? Will he succeed in perpetuating his despotism, and in handing his mighty Empire down to a line of despots like himself?"

A third answered quietly, pointing heavenward:

" 'Behold the Lord, the Lord of hosts, shall lop the bough with terror, and the haughty shall be humbled.' "

* * *

Three months had passed. The regal wedding festivities had far outshone in brilliancy and splendor those of Kings and Emperors born to the purple, and the royal pair had traveled through France and The Netherlands. Their march had been a triumphal one; conquered princes had vied with each other in showing them attentions, and in wishing them happiness.

In midsummer on their arrival in Paris, a ball, the grand finale to the celebrations, was given by the Austrian Ambassador, Prince Schwartzenberg, in the name of the Emperor, Francis II.

An immense hall was built for the purpose. It was hung with curtains and tapestries; a myriad of lights, plants and flowers lent their charm to the fairy scene; the ambassadors, officers, and dignitaries in uniform, with their decorations, and the toilets of the ladies, presented a beautiful picture.

The Empress was quiet but happy, and the Emperor's face beamed with proud self-consciousness and pleasure. His star of fortune was at its zenith. The Empress chatted with the ladies, the Emperor passed from one group of men to another receiving their homage.

Suddenly a giant scheme formed in his brain and shaped itself in a moment, but only an added brilliancy to the light in his eye gave evidence that his ambition was working in new fields. Ambition is never sated.

There was but one who had thwarted him. The Russian Emperor had refused him his daughter in marriage. Him he wished to humble. That done he would be satisfied.

"And—what is there to hinder?" said he to himself. "My power is invincible. My word rules Europe. I *will it*, and nothing is impossible to me."

The cry of "Fire, fire!!" aroused Napoleon from his world of fancies and he looked up to see a thick cloud of smoke through which tongues of flame were leaping.

"Your Majesty, a curtain has caught fire! I fear for the lives of the people!" cried a man to the Emperor.

"The Empress! Where is she?" and Napoleon rushed to her, seized her in his arms and carried her out; none too soon, for when they reached the street, the building was a mass of flames.

"God have mercy on those still within those walls," cried Napoleon looking helplessly about. The Princess Schwartzenberg, sister-in-law of the Ambassador who gave the ball, forced her way through the crowd calling wildly:

"My daughter, who has seen my daughter?" No one answered. The silence was appalling.

"Must she be lost? Will no one help me?" and with these words she rushed into the burning building, forgetting self in her anxiety for her child.

Some men rushed after her, but soon returned to say that they could find neither mother nor daughter.

"Let us go home," said the Empress sick at heart, and Emperor and Empress drove away from the awful scene.

The next morning the Empress said: "Last night I had a fearful dream. I saw you in the midst of a fire in a burning hall, in a burning city; and the fire burned the crown from your head!"

Gloomily Napoleon arose, went to his wife, kissed her gently on the forehead and replied:

"Calm yourself, my darling. That fatal accident last night put those thoughts into your head. My throne and sceptre are more than glittering tinsel, and my house stands on a surer foundation than did that flimsy dance hall put up for the ball."

The Star of Fortune.

A servant entered bringing news of the catastrophe; a countless number had been injured, and many burned and crushed to death in the panic. Among the dead were the mother and daughter of the princely house of Schwartzenberg. The mother had perished in trying to save her child and so badly burned was she, that she was only identified by the jewels that she wore.

Shuddering the young Empress covered her face; the Emperor seemed unmoved. God's warning, "so far shalt thou go and no farther," passed unheeded.

* * *

Two years after this Napoleon's declaration of war against Russia was the talk of Europe, as his grand army began slowly to move eastward and just when he seemed at the very height of earthly power, fire burst from every corner of Moscow, a fire which raged for three days and three nights sweeping everything before it, and with the destruction of Moscow, sank Napoleon's star of fortune, and his hopes of a world empire perished!

Overtaken by reverses and defeats as overwhelming as his successes had been great, exiled, alone, far from home and friends, in the year 1821, his troubled soul passed away.

The Bells of Weyher.

WEYHER, a tiny village in the Palatinate near Landau, is beautifully situated in a valley. From the frowning heights roundabout, four great castles, now in ruins, look down and legend and romance have woven about them many a tale of love and chivalry.

In summer people in search of health flock here, attracted by the mild climate, the enchanting woods and the invigorating air.

In 1794 the French came, drunk with the blood of kings and priests, and insolent in revolutionary intoxication. Churches were no more to them than fine stables, and a handsome residence commanded more respect than the house of God.

After the holy altar the bells of a church are held in veneration throughout Christendom. Their tones are a language fraught with deep significance and human words cannot speak so impressively as do they, in tolling a death knell, in calling the faithful to prayer, in ringing out, "Peace on earth, good-will to men," or in announcing, "Christ Our Lord is risen!"

The Bells of Weyher.

The enemy knowing this wreaked vengeance on the bells, and taking them from the towers, with curses flung them into the mud and dirt of the streets, then gathering the pieces had them cast into cannon. Over all the land the church towers stood sad and silent, and for miles and miles no bells could be heard.

In Weyher they still rang. The iconoclasts had not reached there as yet, but danger threatened, for the French were marching thither, and every one knew that morning would find the enemy in possession of the town.

"They shall not have our bells," cried the people.

"They may rob us of all else, but they shall not take the tongue of belief from our church," and so they counseled how to save their treasures.

In the evening the Burgomaster went to a number of homes and procured eight young men, strong and sturdy fellows, and brave of heart and said to them: "I have called you together to do something for our church, our town; a task for which brave men are needed. What we are about to undertake may cost us our freedom, our lives. I say this that he who fears may leave."

"What is it? Tell us," they cried with one voice.

The Burgomaster answered: "You know me to be an honest man. It is something good and noble—I will tell you what when you have solemnly sworn to die rather than divulge the secret."

"We swear!" cried the villagers.

"Not here. Come to the church. Let us swear before God's high altar, in the flickering light of the lamp in which burns the perpetual fire." Having reached the church the Burgomaster told them his plan of taking the bells from the tower and hiding them until the French were gone.

Solemnly all raised their hands and took the oath:

"We solemnly swear that with God's help, in life or in death, we will reveal to no one where we hide the church bells, nor will we reveal the names of those who do this deed."

Then they knelt before the altar and prayed for success in their undertaking and when they left the church it was almost midnight and darkness enveloped the village.

They procured ropes, chains, necessary implements, and a sled, and work began. With

The Bells of Weyher.

all cautiousness the bells were lowered one by one and placed upon the sled in waiting, and carried into the depths of the woods where on the slope of a hill they were buried. A heavy snow storm completed the work of the burghers.

The French came the next day, and their wrath was indescribable when they found the church tower empty. They hunted through the church, the houses, the cellars — but in vain! To the Burgomaster the commanding officer said:

"Where are the bells? Tell us."

"I do not know," was his truthful reply.

The officer not believing him guiltless in the matter ordered him taken to the Commander-in-chief at Landau. By him he was brutally treated, starved and threatened with death, no word of the secret escaped his lips.

The eight men were questioned, too, but no one betrayed by so much as a syllable the whereabouts of the bells.

The spring storms had swept over the land and the people had told their beads again and again for the Burgomaster, and had given him up for dead, when suddenly he appeared in Weyher. The French were still spying about, but no bells had been found.

One stormy spring day two of the men went to the spot where the bells were buried, and planted vines to mark it for all future time. Unnoticed they went and came. The roots sank into the ground, and the vines grew and twined about the neighboring hawthorn trees, the bells lay silent and thus ten years passed by.

The Burgomaster's hair was fast turning gray, and the young burghers had most of them taken wives to themselves, but for none of them had the chiming of bells announced a wedding fête.

Advent approached and like the Jews of the Old Testament who daily sighed for a Saviour, the people of Weyher daily sighed for their bells.

The Revolution was over; the Palatinate was the inheritance of another and could breathe freely once more. With unspeakable joy was this news received in Weyher.

The Burgomaster called his eight trusty men and gave them orders to get the bells, and the grave, covered with weeds, vines, and overhanging branches, was opened, and the bells, badly rusted, were taken out and carried to the Burgomaster's where they were cleaned and polished until they shone like silver and two days before Christmas they were hung in the tower.

According to custom the villagers were making ready to go to the midnight mass on Christmas Eve. The houses were lighted and dark figures were moving along the street toward the church, when suddenly a mighty clang of bells was heard — a great bell accompanied by smaller ones, chiming joyously in clear, melodious tones.

The voice of these bells was to the people of Weyher like the voice of a parent, of a friend greeting one after long years of separation. Men stood with uncovered heads, windows were thrown open, and from lip to lip passed the happy cry, "The bells! the bells!"

In the church the audience wept tears of joy, and a happier, truer, holier Christmas service has rarely been celebrated than that in the tiny church of Weyher.

On the following day the bells rang for an hour, crying out in joyful harmony: "Glory to God in the highest, peace on earth, goodwill to men," and carrying glad tidings to many a weary, aching heart.

The Saving of St. Damian's.

KAISER Frederick II, the son of Frederick Barbarossa, lay with his army in Pisa threatening to invade Papal territory. Frederick II. was one of the worst rulers the world has ever seen and his hatred of Rome, the Pope, and the Church, his unbelief, and his immorality brought odium against his name. His manner of living was oriental, and his religious views were more Mohammedan than Christian.

The Emperor of the Holy Roman Empire had among his troops many Saracens and words fail to describe the atrocities committed by them in the churches, and monasteries wherever they went.

The people in the cities of Orta, Montefiascone, Sutri, Osimo and Foligno, which lay on their line of march, feared being compelled to surrender either through the power of this army or the treachery of their own inhabitants, and could do naught but wait and watch and pray.

The Saving of St. Damian's.

Not far from Foligno is the ancient Cloister of St. Damian which stands on a high hill surrounded by a thick wall. A very steep path leads up to the entrance gate made of wood with a projecting roof over it.

Inside the walls are the buildings with tiny towers and gables and long galleries. Twenty nuns dwelt within these walls and they were in terror, for on this day three or four hundred of the Saracens were approaching. The bed-ridden abbess who had been helpless for ten years had said to the nuns when the news was brought that the enemy were pillaging the country:

"My children, pray night and day. Pray that God may so blind the Turks that they cannot see our Convent, and will pass us by."

The nuns prayed and fasted, but the Turks came and saw. With loud and triumphant shouts they rushed up the steep pathway, and although the gate creaked and shook beneath their blows it did not give way.

Death would have been a happy release for the poor, frightened, trembling nuns at this moment, as they stood by the bedside of the abbess, weeping and praying.

The abbess suddenly, possessed of supernatural strength, raised herself in bed, stretched out her hand and said:

"Carry me into the church, to the altar."

The nuns obeyed, and from the altar the holy woman took a small pyx, filled with a consecrated wafer, then commanded:

"Carry me to the window over the gate."

The nuns were still more astonished than they had been at her first command, but obeyed, wondering how the bed-ridden abbess could hope to drive away the heathen or to make an impression upon such wicked wretches as those who stormed the Convent.

When the gate did not give way the enemy scaled the walls and dozens of turbaned heads were seen peering over, and the shouting and clamoring was deafening. Just when success seemed to crown their efforts, the abbess, borne by the nuns, appeared holding aloft the holy vessel, and prayed:

"O God, give not the souls of those who know Thee, and serve Thee and whom Thou hast redeemed with Thy precious blood, to these wild beasts."

"I will protect you forever," said a voice in loud commanding tones.

The awful clamoring ceased; in an un-

The Saving of St. Damian's.

wonted terror the enemies dropped from the walls, falling, scrambling, down the precipitous heights, and within a quarter of an hour every Turk had disappeared and St. Damian was saved.

Saint Clara's body is preserved within that building to this day, and countless numbers of pilgrims go every year to St. Damian to see her, the painting commemorating this event, and the ivory pyx which she carried.

SETIS.

LONG before Our Lord and Saviour came to earth, the Holy Ghost swept into the dark and hidden places of heathendom and wherever a soul roused from its lethargy and sleep of sin, there He let fall a ray of godly grace and truth. Not only the people of Judea persevered in the belief in one God and in the hope of a Messiah, but also many pure souls in heathen lands were seized with a presentiment that God must be vastly higher and holier than His creatures, and with this idea grew a secret longing for Him.

Quite two thousand years before Mary and Joseph came to the Nile, fleeing from the wrath of Herod, a calm, clear moonlight gleamed over mighty Memphis. Silent stood the temple with its colossal columns and the smooth faces of the obelisks glittered in the moonlight, and the dull, monotonous swishing of the waters of the Nile was heard throughout the night.

From Pharaoh down to the lowest fellah the weary people slept. In the palace of the

High Priest all was quiet. It had been a hard and busy day, for Pharaoh, the priests and the soldiers of the land had initiated the new god Apis into the Temple.

Apis, the especial favorite of Ra, the most sacred of all the sacred animals worshipped in Egypt, was a black bullock, the first-born, having on his forehead a white mark, on his back another shaped like a sparrow-hawk, on the tail two different kinds of hair, and under the tongue a growth resembling the sacred beetle.

A splendid Temple in Memphis was the abiding place of this god; priests served him daily, and when he died, he was embalmed, and his body was placed in the mausoleum of the temple with great ceremony, while throughout the land there was weeping and wailing until a new Apis was found. That one could ever again find a beast with such markings, to take the place of the one that died, seemed strange and argued that these marks were fraudulent or made by demoniac influence.

For weeks a search was carried on, and a new Apis having been discovered, in a splendid barge, under a golden canopy, the animal was brought to Memphis, and led to his place in the Temple by Pharaoh himself. This day had ended the seven days fête.

In the house of the High Priest some one was still awake, Setis, the daughter of the mighty man. Standing before the open window, she gazed into the garden flooded with moonlight. A soft wind rustled the leaves of the trees, and beyond and above her rose the massive temple of Ra and Apis. As she gazed at it her dark eyes glistened, her lips whispered soft words:

"No, I cannot believe it," and she wrung her hands. "I cannot do as others do, and bow down before this beast. I can pray to the invisible god Ra, but not to this beast. My mother told me that in olden times she was told by her father, the old High Priest, that in the land of the Nile, the people believed in one God only and that then men were better and happier. Now there are many gods and many sacred animals, and men are more wicked and their blessings fewer. Are not all unhappy in the land of Egypt?"—and she sighed, then added:

"Ah! if men dared but speak; and yet I am happy. To-morrow I marry the King's son; then all will be well. But I long for an answer to the questions that torment my soul. O God! tell me what am I? Whither do I go? Who and what and where is Ra? Does he love me? What is there in his worship? My soul craves rest; Where shall I find peace?"

"I will ask Ra himself," she quickly resolved, and throwing her mantle about her, hurried down the stairs and in a few moments was within the temple with a swinging lamp in her hand.

The mighty columns with their painted figures stood like giants before her in the dark, silent, outer room. In an inner room the guards were sleeping, so she pushed back the curtain and entered. The lamps were burning, the golden beams scintillated in ghostly fashion; rugs and garlands hung on the splendid walls; the floors were covered with a purple stuff, and on that reposed the black bullock, chained to the floor.

Setis approached him trembling as she did so.

"What spirit rules here?" she whispered. "I am afraid. Fear fills this room. It is not so without. The good God dwells not here."

Apis lay on the purple rug and stared at her, chewing his cud the while.

"If thou art a god reveal thyself," said the High Priest's daughter.

The beast kept on chewing.

"Infuse into my soul but a gleam of trust and rest and I will believe in thee."

In uncanny stillness Apis lay, a great dark mass.

"And to-morrow am I to come before thee with my bridegroom? And is thy reception of us to be a matter of life or death?

"No, no, I ask nothing of thee," she cried and turned to go.

"I will go to Ra himself," and she went into the inmost part of the temple, the holy of holies. Behind a curtain was the throne of the great god, Ra, but only the High Priest himself was permitted to raise that.

Setis stood still, clasped her hands, raised them heavenwards and offered up a silent prayer. But in vain, the more she prayed, the more tormented was she with fears, for a secret, awful mysterious power seemed to surround her.

"Nothing is of any avail here," she said, "this is no house of holiness, of peace. — I must go."

She passed out of the temple and having

reached her own room, weeping threw herself upon her bed.

"O God, where art Thou? O that I might speak to Thee, that Thou mightst speak to me. I love Thee, for Thee my soul hath longed. I will serve Thee whomsoever Thou art."

Suddenly, as if seized with a divine inspiration, she raised her hands heavenward and cried:

"I pray to Thee, only and invisible God, to Thee, the God, to whom our fathers prayed and wheresoever Thou art, hear me, bless me, I beseech Thee!"

The maid had hardly spoken when her face lighted up, and overjoyed, with a radiant smile on her upturned face, she slowly and reverently sank on her knees. How long she remained there she knew not, for she fell asleep.

In the silent night there came to her a vision. What it was she told no man, but to her weary soul it brought peace, and as morning broke she smiling awoke and made upon her breast the mystic sign of the cross.

Setis appeared in bridal array. Dreamily she stood and waited for the procession headed by the King and her father to approach, the procession that was to lead her and her bridegroom to Apis. Dreamily she moved along, knowing that the reception accorded them would decide her fate; for if it was not propitious no marriage ceremony could take place. There was a low stifled sound that grew louder. Apis was bellowing. Deathly pale the High Priest pulled back the curtain that the procession might pass. Apis rearing and jumping, with flaming eyes and frothing at the mouth, as if possessed of an evil spirit, rushed at Setis from whom all fled, the bridegroom being the first to go. She raised her right hand and silently traced the cross in the air. Apis fell heavily to the floor, panting and gasping.

"Tremble before the cross," said Setis. "Thou art not God, but the wicked spirit of Untruth, and when the true God comes thy kingdom will be here no longer."

King Pharaoh seized Setis. On every side was heard the cry:

"Setis is accursed! The god Apis has gone mad at sight of her! She must die!" Mournfully King Pharaoh repeated the words of the populace: "Cast off by Ra, accursed by Apis, death is thy lot. Thy wedding clothes shall be a winding sheet. Prepare for thy fate."

"Great King, I am ready, and willingly I die. I am unhappy. Earth holds naught for me. I go to find a God of Love, a God of Peace," and clasping her hands, she cried: "Take me, take me, O God, I would be with Thee!"

Setis was led out to be buried alive, her wedding garments her winding sheet. In the charnel house, while the attendants wrapped and bound her she made no struggle, only prayed to the unknown God and traced the mystic sign of the cross in the air. Her hands crossed upon her breast were bound and bands wound about her head and face. The attendants left, their steps echoing and re-echoing on the stone walks, mingling with the sobs and cries of the populace, and growing fainter and fainter, until they were heard no more, and the soul of the martyr Setis passed peacefully to the God of Love.

NOTE. The body of Setis, wrapped in wedding garments and perfectly preserved, was recently discovered by antiquarians.

The Mysterious Voice.

IN the time of the Roman Emperor Domitian a number of men and women were gathered in the home of a distinguished family in Rome. Seated in the open hall they talked earnestly. Two men of noble bearing formed the centre of the group, to whom the others listened with wrapt attention, for they spoke of the Christians, repeating the terrible accusations made against them, and also the praiseworthy things done by them.

A young man named Linus remarked:

"The things one hears about the Christians are the things told by the Christians themselves. They may invent many of the tales but I have yet to hear any of these wonderful things from men who worship gods. Evidence from them would be more convincing."

"I will tell you something," said the elder of the two men, "that will convince you. When the Emperor Tiberius lived, a ship bearing passengers of many nationalities, sailed from Greece to Italy. One evening as the

The Mysterious Voice.

vessel approached an island, Paxos by name, the wind went down and the sea became very calm, the stars one by one came out, the people sat on the deck eating and drinking and enjoying the scene.

Suddenly from the still waters there arose a strange, deep voice, calling 'Thamus.'

'Who calls the pilot?' cried the people for all had heard his name distinctly.

The pilot, Thamus, an Egyptian, had heard the call, too, and was trying to appear indifferent, but could ill conceal his uneasiness.

Thinking it an illusion, the people began chatting when again, and this time with awful clearness, from out the deep came the call, 'Thamus.' Terror and confusion seized the people, and the pilot turned pale and did not answer thinking it his death call. The silence was appalling.

After a few moments, for a third time, the voice was heard, calling louder than before and almost threateningly. Trembling in every limb the pilot rose and answered:

'Thamus is here. What is wanted.'

'When you pass by Palodes, you are to announce that great Pan is dead!'

All heard the answer plainly; deep sadness

seemed to possess the speaker and consternation was depicted on every face. The pilot thought much concerning his commission: 'What could it mean? Who was dead? Who was great Pan? Whence this mysterious voice? Was it one of the gods that had died?'

To his vain questioning he found no answer.

The next day at noon the shore of Palodes rose before them. Mountains and wood lay in the distance enveloped in blue haze. The winds went down, and the sails flapped lazily in the noonday sun. Awful sadness had settled on all nature, and weighed heavily on the hearts of the travelers.

The pilot stepped to the ship's side, and tried to raise his voice, but could not at first, but mastering his fears, he finally shouted to the lonely isle, 'Great Pan is dead! Great Pan is dead!'

Death seemed on every side. The sea was calm, not even the plashing of the water against the vessel's side could be heard, the sun became obscured, darkness settled over all, a darkness that lasted for some time. Then followed a great trembling of the land and water, the waves dashed mountain high, and in the midst of this disturbance, voices

The Mysterious Voice.

repeated the cry, 'Great Pan is dead! Great Pan is dead!' softly at first, then louder and louder, as if thousands were wailing, then came one fearful, shrill prolonged cry that rose from heaven to earth, 'Great Pan is dead!'

All nature seemed with one accord to give expression to grief, and the cries, like the wailings of lost souls, died on the breeze.

The wind arose, the sails filled, and the journey was continued. The frightened travelers calmed their fears, but could give no explanation of what had occurred, while none doubted that it presaged some direful thing.

Without further demonstrations they reached Rome and recounted the news, which finally reached the ears of the Emperor Tiberius, who ordered Thamus to come before him. The recital of the Egyptian made a deep impression on him and he continued his inquiries, without, however, reaching any definite conclusion.

Some little time passed and the Emperor Tiberius went to his villa in Capri, near Naples, and there news was brought to him from his Governor in Palestine, that the King of the Jews, Jesus of Nazareth, had been crucified. The report dwelt upon the life and death of Jesus and the date of the crucifixion tallied with that of the remarkable experience of the travelers at sea.

The enigma was solved for the Emperor at least, but he never made public his thoughts on the subject. The Senate, however, was ordered to number the crucified Jesus among the Roman gods."

"And who really was meant by 'Great Pan'?" asked Linus when the speaker had stopped.

"We Christians give two explanations. One is, that this was an announcement of the death of Our Lord, who on that day died on the cross, and as the earth shook in Palestine, and day was turned to night, so here the sea and the islands gave expression to sadness because of the death of their Creator.

"The other is, that when Jesus died he conquered hell and the gods whom men had worshipped, and the cries heard were the cries of the lost bemoaning their fate. Jesus died to rise again, but the spirits of hell are lost forever, sunk in the vast abysses beneath the earth."

"But," interrupted Linus, "may not those be tales invented by the Christians?"

The Mysterious Voice.

"No, Linus; you know the historian Plutarch, who was not a Christian? Read his account of the stopping of the oracles and you will find this story. Thamus, the Egyptian died only a short time ago and there are people living now who were on that ship. Plutarch mentions one in particular, Epitherses, the father of Aemilianus whom we all know to be incapable of speaking falsely."

"Epitherses," cried Linus, "the father of the rhetorician Aemilianus? I know him well, and I would believe his every word."

"Very well. Let him be your witness. He is a Christian," said another.

"I will go to him and learn the Christian precepts," said Linus.

"You do not need to go to him," said the wife of Linus quietly, "I can teach you, for I am a Christian."

Looking at her with astonishment, he cried taking her by the hand: "You a Christian! Teach me of this unknown God who can shake the earth and disturb the very sea's depths. Be he Pan or Christus, I would know him."

The Saying of the Oracle.

LONG ago, close by the Bay of Naples, lay the city of Pompeii, its beautiful homes embedded in bowers of roses, groves of orange and laurel, while picturesquely behind it in the distance rose the mountains.

On one day the people had gone to the Circus early, and although an intermission had been granted, most of them had preferred to remain in their places to be sure of seeing the Christian martyrs fight the wild beasts.

In a beautiful home in the heart of the town was a small group of people, grandfather, granddaughter and slave, that had not been attracted to this scene, and in the inner court where a fountain plashed, and flowers grew, protected from the sun by awnings, the three reposed in the refreshing shade.

"What of Vesuvius to-day, Syrus? Is the eruption over?" asked the old man of the slave in a high thin voice.

"No reliable news is to be had master," responded the slave. "No one dares approach

The Saying of the Oracle.

very near and from the town nothing can be seen but clouds of smoke and steam."

"Go pray to the gods, Syrus, for our safety," said the old man and to his grandchild Domitilla he added:

"Last night, child, when the earth shook, and Vesuvius sent forth flames an occurrence of my youth came to mind."

"Oh, what was it, grandfather," cried Domitilla.

"Domitilla, my parents as you know, dwelt in the Alban Mountains and I was brought up there after a different fashion from the one of to-day. To-day it is the boast of Roman youths to know all pleasures and vices, and to despise the gods: in my day it was my pride to live spotlessly and honorably and to love and honor the gods, my parents and the truth. When I had grown to manhood I came to Naples but before starting on my journey I consulted an oracle regarding my future.

"The oracle was in a cave near the top of a high mountain and there, too, dwelt a soothsayer."

"O grandfather, don't talk so slowly, hurry! I want to hear about it," interrupted the girl.

"It was a dreadful place, wild and desolate;

giant rocks lay on every side; in places the light of heaven was almost shut out by overhanging rocks, from others greenish yellow smoke issued. There were few plants and trees, and here and there crawled snakes, which I dared not kill for fear of desecrating the place. Having come to the soothsayer's cave I trembled so that I dared not call her. Suddenly an ugly old woman stood before me, her gray hair blowing about her face, her eyes dull and sunken, and she asked who I was and wherefore I came.

I gave her a rich present that I had brought with me and said that I wished to consult the oracle before starting upon my journey. Commanding me to wait she disappeared and I waited a long, long time. The sun went down and it grew very cold for it was winter time.

Finally the old woman returned and led me into a tiny cave, the sight of which caused me to shudder. There were brilliant spots of light on the walls that shone but dimly on account of the hazy smoke which filled the place, and in the middle sat a maiden, her head bowed and supported by both hands, her face deathly pale. Now and then she trembled, wrung her hands, groaned and sighed as if in greatest agony of mind.

The Saying of the Oracle. 61

'Do not disturb her,' commanded the old woman. 'Wait until she questions you.'

I obeyed and after an hour or more the maid in a shrill unnatural voice asked whence I had come? I answered her, and she bent down to earth and prayed and listened.

The old woman encouragingly whispered: 'Now she will tell you all you wish to know?'

The maid rose and turned her face to me, her eyes were closed, she seemed entranced, I hardly dared breathe for fear of losing some word, then suddenly she gave a fearful scream, fell over, quickly raised herself, opened her eyes, and stood very still and rigid. Following her eyes, I saw through a fissure in the cave's roof a beam of light, bright as sunshine, a star, the largest and most brilliant I had ever seen.

The sight of this was overpowering to her, she quite forgot me, her face lighted up with a look of unspeakable joy and peace, then as if seized by some unseen power, she fell, wildly calling: 'Help! help!'

I tried to help her but the old woman would not let me do so. Again she cried: 'Help, save me from the god of the Nether Regions. Free me. I will no longer be his priestess?'

Sounds, fearful and prolonged, like the cries of thousands of wild beasts, resounded and reverberated through the mountains.

I held the maid as she lay swooning, not daring to move. The old woman shrieked, then all was still.

Finally the maid rousing said:

'I see you; a slave teaches you, a maid gives you greatest riches, a death brings you life. Flee and never return here. Fearful has been this night.'

I fled, amazed, terrified, and told my parents all that I had seen. My father went the next day to investigate the place and found the old woman dead in the cave, but the soothsayer had disappeared."

"How dreadful, grandfather!" cried Domitilla.

"Last night those predictions came to mind, but I must put such thoughts aside. I am nearly a hundred years old and my days are drawing to an end and I know not—"

"Only see, grandfather, — the birds are seeking shelter under our portico! Hear how they chatter and the dogs are barking and howling!" cried Domitilla.

It grew darker and darker, fearful rumb-

The Saying of the Oracle. 63

lings were heard, in the streets people were running and screaming, the sky grew very light, then darkened.

"This is a terrible storm," said the grandfather. "May the gods preserve us," and he turned to the Penates to pray.

The slave came from the corner where he had been listening very attentively to the conversation and said:

"Master, I have served you faithfully all my life long, grant me one favor?"

"It is granted, but you ask at an unseasonable hour; to-morrow, Syrus," replied the old man.

"To-morrow may be too late," replied the slave. "My request concerns you. Allow me to explain the saying of the oracle, which was told you in your youth."

The old man looked up in astonishment and murmuring softly, "a slave teaches you," nodded assent saying, "Hurry, a storm seems to be coming."

"You are fortunate, O Master, in that you were a witness of the greatest, the most mysterious night, the world has ever seen. On that night of which you spoke, the Saviour of man was born, the Prince of Peace, for whom the world was waiting and who brings peace and happiness. The star you saw was no ordinary star."

"That is true," interrupted the old man, "I saw it when I fled from the cave down the mountain, and such a wonder in the heavens has not been seen since."

"It was the star foretold by the prophets of old, that heralded Christ's coming. All peoples saw it and were assured, and no wonder the sibyl in the cave was excited, for by that she was freed from the spirits of the Nether World. The oracle of which you speak was not the only one silenced on that night. In many places wonderful things took place; to Augustus, Christ appeared that night, in Rome pure oil sprang from the ground and flowed three days then stopped and—"

With a gesture of his hand the old man commanded Syrus to stop speaking and asked:

"What is the name of this one and only God of earth who was on that night born?"

The slave answered: "Jesus Christ."

"And are you a Christian?" asked the old man.

The slave knelt beside his master and said: "Yes, through God's grace, and Master, you have given to your slave the honor of bringing to you the message of truth."

"You — a Christian, Syrus," slowly repeated the master and throwing his head back he swooned.

Domitilla screamed, "Help, Syrus!" the earth shook, quantities of hot ashes fell, great stones came down striking the earth with a terrific noise, the waves lashed the shore, the lava hissed as it poured into the sea, and there were groans and cries on every side.

With difficulty a torch was lighted and through the court, and atrium, already covered with ashes a foot deep, the slave and maid were bearing the swooning man to the cellar, when at the entrance they found people forcing themselves into the house carrying a young girl on a litter.

Putting her down one man said:

"Here she may die in peace, we can carry her no farther."

"Out with her she is a Christian!" cried others. "Let the horses in the street trample her to death!"

The noise roused the master, and he said: "This is my house. The Christian is under my protection. Begone!" Syrus and the watch dog enforced the command.

Syrus had greeted the two men as they entered and now that the noise had subsided, asked whom they carried on the litter.

Diakon looking earnestly at the slave replied:

"One who much desires to see you." Gazing attentively at the prostrate figure in the dim light he recognized his daughter, and with a cry of surprise and anguish he said:

"Miriam, my child, why the blood on your clothes? What accident has befallen you?"

Miriam was past speaking, so Diakon explained:

"Your daughter is a martyr. Yesterday it was discovered that she was a Christian, and to-day at the Circus she was brought into the arena to be torn to pieces by wild beasts. A bear fell upon her and was about to devour her just when Vesuvius burst forth. The beast hearing the awful sounds fled terrified and we saved the maid. She is mortally wounded but wished us to bring her to you. She could say no more."

Miriam opened her eyes, looked about and tried to speak, but could not.

With great effort she raised her hand to her bosom, and took out a tiny gold box containing consecrated bread. By her look she seemed to ask for the blessed sacrament, which she was past receiving. Her hand fell limply to her side; a sweet smile and the martyr's soul passed away.

Weeping the slave threw himself on the body of his beloved child, and in deepest awe the little group gazed at father and daughter.

Outside the air was thick with ashes which were fast burying the city and there was naught to do but await the inevitable.

At last Syrus roused himself, took the bread from the tiny box, and after baptizing the master and Domitilla, using water in the place of wine Diakon administered the sacrament to all, and as they prayed the old man murmured: "A slave teaches you, a maid gives you greatest riches, a death brings you life!"

The Vestal Virgins.

THE sun sank in radiant splendor in the west lighting with golden hues the Temple of Vesta. Night was settling down on Imperial Rome, magnificent in architectural beauties, Pagan Rome where with feasting and dancing, song and laughter, the fêtes of the heathen gods were celebrated in street and palace and temple.

Of all Rome's temples none was more beautiful, though many were far more magnificent than the Temple of Vesta, on the shore washed by the yellow Tiber's wave. Its tall pillars of dazzling whiteness supported a dome-shaped roof and within was a tiny cella shut out from the world, upon whose low stone altar burned the sacred fire. Clothed in flowing robes of white, six priestesses of the goddess Vesta, maidens chosen from the noblest families of Rome, guarded this sacred fire and kept it ever burning.

Their vow of chastity and service to Vesta was for thirty years, after which time they could return to the world.

The Vestal Virgins.

All Rome looked upon these maidens with greatest awe and veneration and many were the privileges granted them. In the amphitheatre their place was next to the Emperor. When on the street they were escorted by their own guard, and theirs was the power to grant pardon to any criminal condemned to death, whom they chanced to meet, but death was the inevitable fate of her who broke the vow of chastity.

As the night wore on the Vestal Virgin sat before the altar with her face buried in her hands; in her heart a sacred foreboding, a sad uncertainty, and the whispered communion that she held with self was echoed by the white marble walls.

"Is it true that there is no life after death? What awaits us in the future? Does death end all? Is the sweet dream of a time to come when all will be unspeakable joy, but a delusion of my fancy? My heart yearns for happiness, but where is it to be found? The things about me, the gods, are terrible. I feel myself drawn by an unseen power and my soul is full of longing for a God of Love."

The walls gave no reply.

"O God, whoever and wherever thou art,

give me of Thy peace, free my soul of its longings, its vague desires. The world, its pomps and vanities are naught to me. O God, be my good Father, love and cherish Thy child."

The Vestal Virgin gave way to her grief in loud cries. Suddenly a voice said, "Dear one, be comforted!" and looking she saw there in the Temple of Chastity, the form of a lovely woman with a child clasped in her arms.

She appeared in bright effulgence, clad in a robe of shimmering white, a blue veil interwoven with silver wrapped about her, upon her head a crown of stars of dazzling brilliancy.

Overcome with her own unworthiness and humility she hardly dared gaze into the calm peaceful eyes of mother and child. Fear left her soul, in this vision she found the fulfilment of her desires.

A voice seemed to say:

"Remain as thou art, pure in heart, devote thyself to the God whom thou hast not seen, be humble, repent thy sins, flee the world and its lusts, live and hope for a future life. Morning dawns. The morning for which the world longs is come, the morning when one God shall rule, before whom the gods of this world shall bow in the dust.

"In this Temple soon the sacred fire will be extinguished, and the Temple that has for two hundred years seen the worship of the goddess Vesta, will for two thousand years and more, in fact, so long as it stands, witness the worship of the true God."

The figures disappeared, the maid was alone before the altar upon which the fire was dim and smoldering. Throwing herself upon the floor, she wept bitterly that the heavenly vision had vanished, the vision which had blessed her.

The most quiet, the most pious, the most stainless of all the Vestal Virgins, from that time on devoted herself to the unknown God. Her thirty years of service to Vesta were almost over, and she was trembling at the thought of her return to the world. Her anxiety, however was unnecessary, for just before the completion of the time of service, she fell ill and died, a sweet smile upon her lips.

Upon Rome's hills in picturesque ruins lie the palaces of her Christian Emperors; by the rushing Tiber's wave, with these massive sentinels guarding it, still stands the little Temple of Vesta, now a Christian Chapel.

Over the entrance is a picture of the Blessed Virgin holding the Christ Child, with the sun beneath her feet,—the Vestal Virgin's vision preserved on canvas to comfort, and inspire mankind, as it once did the heathen maid, watching the sacred fire within the heathen sanctuary. A sacred fire still flames in that same chapel, the perpetual fire burning before the Christian altar, telling that the Host is present, the God of gods, the Lord of heaven and earth.

THE KISS OF THE CHRIST CHILD.

MORE than four hundred years ago in the cloister of the Clarisses at Bologna, there lived a nun now honored as a saint in all churches. The world knew nothing or very little of her. When about fourteen years of age she was often seen as a companion of a Princess belonging to a well-known Bolognese family, and more admiring glances were cast upon her than upon the Princess.

One day she disappeared, and was never seen again by the eyes of the world. When anyone inquired after the maiden whose future seemed to promise so much, people pointed with a silent gesture to the cloister, that rose stern and foreboding in the midst of the city. Behind these walls through whose gates no man had ever passed, and out of which no nun had ever returned to the world, lived the bride of Christ, free and spotless, in prayer and meditation, — as once St. John may have lived in the desert,—a mysterious life of communion with God and the Holy Ghost.

The maid had been here for a number of years, the happiest of all the nuns, having found sweet peace, the peace that the world can not give. But she was not forgotten by the outside world.

One evening a noisy crowd of young men were passing the convent, men of good social standing, but noisy and loud in their merry-making. Bologna has to-day the reputation of being the most turbulent of all the Italian cities, and so it was four hundred years ago when it was the seat of the most celebrated University in the world, and contained wicked, disorderly, godless men.

The company went to the convent and stood outside its quiet, stern walls laughing and joking. Two in particular became much excited and one said to the other jeeringly:

"Why do you not serenade your bride who is behind those walls?"

The companion replied with an oath that ill concealed his feelings.

"My bride? Why do you scoff? That woman has poisoned my life. I intended having her for my wife and—"

"Did you tell her your desires and intentions?" said the first.

The Kiss of the Christ Child. 75

"No"—was the hesitating reply. "I don't know as I ever said anything about marriage, but I've sworn my enmity to her nevertheless," replied the second moodily.

"And why, Hothead? How could she possibly know your intentions if you never told them to her parents or to her?"

"She ought to be my wife instead of being in that cloister," he continued in the same strain. "I wanted her and made up my mind to have her, and she thwarted all my plans."

"You are unreasonable, my friend. She knew nothing of your wishes when she went into the cloister, so intentionally she did nothing to poison your life. Why talk so? She is better off now for she is the bride of Christ. Life with you surely could not be so peaceful as the one she enjoys."

An oath was the reply and the controversy continued, but the companions wearying of the talk of the blasphemers left them. The man giving vent to his rage and allowing himself to become wrought to a frenzy, beat with his fists against the walls, screamed and uttered all sorts of vain threats.

Not so much as a shadow darkened the windows above. During this scene the nun

Katherine knelt in her cell, having no intimation of what was going on outside the walls of the cloister. She did not even know this man who had never sought her hand in marriage, much less did she know of his presence and while he raged, in calm, serene, sublime majesty and sweetness the Blessed Virgin bearing the Christ Child in her arms appeared before the saintly nun, as she knelt praying. Katherine raised her pure eyes and the words that passed between mother and son were heard only by her. All was so sacred, so holy, that the nun felt herself in heaven and when they started to go she held the Child by the hand in reverential awe. He bent over and said:

"I will give to you an imperishable token," embraced her and kissed her on the lips. She was in a transport of joy that such bliss should be vouchsafed her, and when she calmed herself, the blasphemer had gone.

Four hundred years and more have passed over Bologna and the Cloister of the Clarisses since that time. The blasphemer is dead, his body long since mouldered to dust, his name forgotten, and God only knows what has become of his immortal soul.

And Katherine the nun? In the Chapel of the Cloister of the Clarisses sits Saint Katherine just where she has sat these four hundred years. The grave gave up her body, death had no power over her; as she was in life so she is now, her body still retains the flesh. In quiet, peaceful, silent majesty she rests in the garb of her order. Her features and hands are discolored with age; but, upon her lower lip is a clear, bright spot, a spot that has remained through the years, the imprint of the kiss of the Christ Child.

The Artist of the Bregenz Wood.

IN a tiny village picturesquely situated near the Bregenz Forest in Switzerland, one evening long ago, a woman prayed before the altar of a deserted church. Her heart was sad and lonely, for she was constantly separated from her husband, an artist, who did church decorations and painted religious pictures.

Their eldest daughter, Angelica, inherited the father's talent, and it became the aim and ambition of his life to make of her a great painter. When scarcely seventeen years of age he took her to Italy where she painted portraits of illustrious people under his guidance. The separation from the daughter added fresh sorrow to the mother who remained at home, sometimes for months at a time, with the younger children.

When Angelica and her father received a commission to decorate the village church and returned home after an absence of a year and a half, the mother rejoiced greatly. Their visit, however, was a short one and after their departure she had their work to solace her in her loneliness.

Seated in the church gazing at the pictures of the saints, which they had painted on the walls, the thought that those nearest and dearest to her had created these forms of wondrous beauty, caused her eyes to fill with tears as she prayed:

"O dear saints in heaven, and thou, O Blessed Virgin, whose honor and fame my dear child's brush has served to promote, take her under thy watchful care and let thy protection be her reward."

Angelica had been gone a long time in the far away English capital, and had written that she would remain there for an indefinite time, but that the father would return shortly. She had been befriended by a distinguished family, had been introduced to a number of influential people and had obtained many commissions to paint portraits.

"A young woman alone in London! My daughter alone in that great city!" sighed the mother's troubled heart, and she prayed long and fervently:

"Mother of God, keep my child."

A few years passed and Angelica Kauffmann,

the modest child of the Bregenz Forest had become the pet of London society, honored and loved. Marked attentions were shown her on every side and many were the commissions for portraits that she received from royalty. She was admitted to the Academy, an extraordinary mark of favor, and received large sums of money for her work.

One afternoon in the month of May, a distinguished young man was announced, Count Horn, a member of a noble Swedish family. After a very short call he left the salon of the artist with beaming face, and Angelica went to her boudoir.

The long mirror reflected her graceful figure, her flushed cheeks, her brilliant eyes dark and sparkling with excitement. Turning from the mirror she went to the window overlooking the garden, but she did not see the beautiful flowers, the trees in foliage, nor did she hear the birds singing, she felt only the refreshing breeze.

She had just accepted Count Horn and they were soon to marry. For a long time he had paid her marked attentions, and his knightly bearing, his charming manners, and witty conversation had won her heart. He had

The Artist of the Bregenz Wood. 81

asked that the engagement be kept a secret, and she had agreed though unwillingly. "To prevent gossip," was the reason he gave. She stood at the window a long time absorbed in thought for she was sorely troubled. Her conscience said to her: "You have not consulted your parents; you have not spoken to the Count about his religion; you have not been to confession; you have not advised with those capable of counseling you on the subject of marriage but have followed merely your own whims and desires in the matter."

She drew a deep sigh and continued gazing out of the window.

Angelica would gladly have sought advice and changed her mind had she seen Count Horn at this moment in close conference with Sir Joshua Reynolds, Director of the Academy. Reynolds was her bitter enemy. He envied her her ability and her fame and wished to humble her. He had offered himself to her in marriage not from love of her but from malignant motives, hoping to get her within his power. Piqued by her refusal he schemed against her in other ways.

Angelica Kauffmann and Count Horn were secretly married, the witnesses being friends chosen by the Count. Shortly after this the great painter Reynolds gave a ball to which a countless number of lords and ladies of high rank were bidden. Count Horn told his wife that he wished her to go, and that at this ball their marriage was to be announced officially. She raised no objections. They arrived very late. The host presented them to the guests as Count and Countess Horn, and Angelica noticed the sarcastic smile that played on the lips of Reynolds each time that he referred to her by her new title. She also noticed the peculiar manner in which some of the guests looked at her husband, the whisper that passed from lip to lip, and she, the petted idol of London society found herself standing with her husband, in the center of the brilliantly lighted room, the circle about them growing wider and wider.

A stately gentleman of noble bearing came forward. There was silence. She felt her husband tremble when he bowed in acknowledgement of the introduction, "Count Horn allow me to present the Count and Countess Horn."

"Ah, are we relatives?" very politely questioned the stranger, looking straight at the

Countess' husband who let go of her arm and took a step backward. The stranger took him by the hand saying at the same time to the Countess:

"This man is your husband, do you say?"

"Certainly," she replied, seized with an awful presentiment of ill to come.

"And you are really married to him?"

"Yes, truly, six weeks ago," she answered mechanically.

"And this man, your husband, does he call himself Count Horn?"

Angelica could no longer control herself and cried in desperation:

"What is the meaning of this? Do you wish to kill me or to drive me mad? So far as I know, my husband, this man whom I married six weeks ago is Count Horn!"

"Rascal, whom do you pretend to be? You are my discharged valet. I am Count Horn, the only person bearing that title," and he grasped his hand more firmly.

"Your Lordship, your Lordship, have mercy!" cried the imposter, while the true Count Horn, with a cane brought him for the purpose cudgeled the man before the assembled company.

Angelica Kauffmann, the proud artist, the darling of the Court, the wife of a discharged valet!

As she stood speechless with amazement, her face pale, her features set, Reynolds came up to her and whispered in sarcastic tone:

"I congratulate you on your taste, Countess." Her pale lips could utter no reply, and without a word she fell in a dead faint.

Zucchi, an Italian artist, stepped forward and placing himself before Reynolds said:

"Ladies and gentlemen, the valet, who has been shown to be an imposter is a low villain, but there is a much lower villain here our host, Director Reynolds who planned this scene," and with these words he struck Reynolds a blow full in the face, and walked out of the room.

Angelica's dream of happiness was at an end; her popularity went like a bubble, and there was no one but herself to be blamed for her misfortunes. The imposter who was paid by Reynolds for the part he took in the drama was punished and disappeared, the marriage annulled.

The friends of the days when Angelica's star was in the ascendancy proved false.

Alone in the world, she realized the vanity of all things human, and that, only in duty, is true happiness to be found.

Later she married Antonio Zucchi, and in Italy, they lived and worked together happily. Angelica Kauffmann was to her husband what her name indicates, little angel, and after having experienced life's bitterness, its joys came to them like manna from heaven.

The Meeting.

ON Christmas Eve in a tiny house in one of the suburbs of Vienna, a sturdy young man and his wife were busy putting the last touches to a Christmas tree.

The Christmas tree was small and mean. On its branches were seven candles, a few apples, a dozen or more gilded nuts, and a tiny angel of marzipan; from the top fluttered strips of paper of different colors, and narrow silk ribbons were wound about it. All these things showed wear for they had been used many times before. There were no presents. When the husband had lighted the seventh little candle, his wife opened the door and called the children.

What joy! They danced and clapped their hands and laughed and shouted.

The poor little candles, the apples and nuts had for them the magic witchery of priceless treasures. Each candle, each shining nut, each twig was examined, and each object was a new pleasure to them.

The Meeting.

Tears were in the mother's eyes when she opened the door to usher in the children to their Christmas festivities for they had never before been so poor and mean. The children, however, were happy and content, and offered no word of complaint or criticism, and their pleasure recalled to the parents their youth and happier days, and they felt themselves children once more with their children, and all joined in singing: "O Holy Night."

As they were about to begin the second verse a knock was heard. In response to the surprised, half-frightened, "Come in," of the father, the door opened and a tall, distinguished looking woman entered. A long mantle enveloped her figure and a thick black veil covered her face.

For a moment she looked about the tiny room, and then asked, "Am I at the home of Bernard, the cabinet maker?"

"I am Bernard, Madam," said the father.

"May I speak with you a moment?"

"Yes, certainly," and the wife came forward with a friendly greeting.

"I know I seem to be intruding," began the stranger, "but what I wish to question you about is for your best interest. Trust me. Have you any work?"

The man responded with a deep sigh, "Yes, — but I make nothing from it." His wife started to speak, tears rolled down her face and she cried out, "Oh, the Jew! the Jew! For six months he has had us in his power. We owed him money and we have paid it ten times over, but he always finds some new obligation. Day and night he torments my husband, and what we get by toil and care, and saving, week after week goes to the Jew. My husband does nothing but work for him, and yet is all the time fearful of being sued by him for debt.

"O how happy we used to be! — and now? We are poor as church mice."

Very much moved the stranger listened to this recital.

"You must allow me one question. What is the name of your creditor?"

The husband took a slip of paper from the desk and gave it to her, saying:

"There is his address. You can question about him. Our neighbors, the Sisters of the Good Shepherd, can bear witness that my wife has often been to them in our trouble."

"I quite understand," interrupted the woman and fearing she had spoken too abruptly,

The Meeting.

she asked, "How much is the debt, may I ask?"

"One hundred twenty gulden," replied the man slowly, and his head sunk on his breast. There was a pause.

"If some one were to loan you the hundred twenty gulden, without interest, but subject to recall at a certain time, would it be of any assistance to you?"

The poor cabinet-maker and his wife stood speechless with amazement. Tears came to his eyes and in a choking voice he said:

"In God's name, I beg you not to trifle with the sorrows of the poor on this holy night. We cannot expect such good fortune as that."

The woman drew out her purse and said, "Write me out a receipt for one hundred twenty gulden. There is the money," and handing it to the wife, added, "Count and see if it is right." The wife seized the small beautiful hand of the stranger and kissed it, while tears of joy streamed down her face. "Come children, come quickly, and thank the lady for her goodness."

In a moment she was surrounded as if by magic by five blooming children, who seized her hands and kissed them and looked up to her lovingly, trying in every possible way to express gratitude.

The four-year old Rudolph interested the woman particularly. She took him in her arms and kissed him and he tried with his bright eyes to peep through her veil.

The father handed her his note saying: "Here is my note. Look at it and see if it is correct. The writing is poor. I was hardly able to write for joy. May God reward you a thousand times over in this world and in the world to come. You have saved my family and me. O Theresa," turning to his wife, "how happy we are now and what a Christmas!" then turning again to his benefactress added: "Madam, you have saved us. We all promise to pray for you."

"Rudolph," she said to the boy whom she still held in her arms, "which is your candle on the Christmas tree?"

Boldly Rudolph pointed to the nearest one. Handing the child the note and going closer to the poor little tree, she said:

"Hold it up over the candle."

He did so and in a moment let the flaming paper drop from his hand.

The Meeting. 91

"Well done! There is something for the Christmas tree," she said, laying a gold piece on the table, and putting Rudolph down she quickly walked to the door.

He held her by the dress and said: "O dear lady, let me whisper something to you."

She bent over to listen, but could not understand him, so said sweetly, "What is it, my little one? Speak louder."

"Let me see your face," cried the boy and the family joined in the request.

The stranger hesitated a moment, then realizing that interest and gratitude rather than curiosity actuated them, raised her veil for a moment, and seven pairs of eyes gazed at a radiantly beautiful young face of extraordinary delicacy with a mass of golden hair about it.

Calling out, "God bless you and watch over you," she hurriedly disappeared in the darkness.

"Where have I seen that face before?" musingly questioned Bernard. "I'll *never, never* forget it."

* * *

Death had visited the royal palace. The lackeys, the soldiers, the house-servants attired in deepest mourning, were directing the crowd that had come to pay a last tribute to the dead.

In the palace hall filled with incense, a countless number of candles were burning around the catafalque on which lay in state the body of the young Archduchess Elizabeth.

She was like a beautiful wax image; her hands were folded on her breast, her eyes were closed, about her mouth there played a faint happy smile, and from beneath the wreath of roses on her head shone a wealth of golden hair.

Motionless, cold and still lay this earthly veil of a pure soul, unconscious of what was going on about her, seeing neither the tears of the mourners, nor hearing the words of praise of those who gazed upon her.

Officers stood beside the catafalque as guard of honor, two Capuchin monks, knelt a little to one side praying for the soul of the departed as the long line of people filed through the hall.

Bernard, the cabinet-maker was among the number. His little son, Rudolph, had begged so hard to come that to please him, the father had brought him, and so that he might see better he held him in his arms.

The Meeting.

"Papa, papa! our beautiful lady!" he cried, and his childish voice rang out through the silence of the hall. Bernard stood motionless before the figure, with great tears rolling down his cheeks.

"O God, give thee eternal rest," he whispered, "if I could awaken thee, I would do so with my heart's blood."

"Pass on. People are not allowed to stand," cried an officer, and Bernard was pushed along by the crowd. He saw nothing more, for his eyes were swimming with tears, but he had found and recognized his benefactress and savior—on her death-bed.

Note. True story of the Archduchess Elizabeth of Austria.

A Cheering Word.

TWO journeymen sat at a table in a humble little inn in an Alpine village. Each had a small glass of gin, a half bottle of thin yellow must and a piece of coarse black bread before him.

It was midwinter and bitterly cold, the snow creaked as they walked, and a sharp wind from the northeast swept through the valley. The young men were poorly protected against the wintry blasts for their clothing was thin, their coats short (they had no overcoats); around their necks were scarfs that once had served as neckties, and about their ears they had wrapped colored handkerchiefs. They ate and drank slowly that they might stay as long as possible in the comfortably warmed room.

One, taking his purse from his pocket, said to the old innkeeper who sat in the room with them:

"What is our bill?"

"Fifteen pfennig for each," was the reply. "There is no charge for the bread."

A Cheering Word. 95

"You will pay it?" asked the other, and the companion responded: "Certainly and I have yet enough for some cheese. We'll divide the money."

"Is that all the money you have?" asked the innkeeper.

"Not a single piece more," replied the man, "but I'm not much troubled about that, for I will be at home by noon. I live in Thäle. My mother has there a home for me, and I'll find the money there which I earned during the summer and sent home to her for safe keeping. She is better at saving than I," and he laughed.

"Are you a stucco-worker?" asked the innkeeper.

"Yes and my companion also. He has farther to go than I, for his home is near Aalen.

"God protect you from the cold," said the old man sympathetically.

"There, take your pfennigs. If it were not so early in the day I should insist on your remaining over night. The birds drop from the trees in weather like this."

"Oh, I'll soon be at home!" said the second cheerily.

"I have good blood in my body and can walk along at a quick pace. I can reach Algenfeld to-day, and there I know a good inn, where the landlady will keep me over night."

"Adieu, God bless you and watch over you!"

"Thank you very much for all your kindness to us," said the first as they put their knapsacks on their backs. "You speak like a priest."

"Oh, I'm not a priest, but I have learned much of priestly ways from the Bishop," was the good old man's reply.

"From the Bishop?" queried the men in surprise. "Has he ever stopped here with you?"

"No, not exactly, but his last pastoral letter which was read from the pulpit by the priest, contained instructions which I have heeded and shall till my dying day."

"And what did he say?"

"A kind word to a fellow mortal is often of greater value than hard gold."

The journeymen laughed cheerily.

"That would be a cheap way of giving alms," said the one, the other added: "To me a piece of gold would be of more value that a hundred kind words."

The old man said earnestly:

A Cheering Word. 97

"Do not joke about the Bishop's words, for he knows what is right and Christian better than all the white-washers of Thäle put together. He did not say one should give fine words to the poor instead of alms, but that one ought not to throw one's alms behind one like meat to a dog."

"You are quite right, mine host," said both together.

"It is a pleasing thought and the world would be better if people would act upon it.

"God bless you for it and good-by."

The two resumed their journey. The way to Thäle is long, especially in winter time; night comes on early and thick clouds settle down increasing the cold.

At the end of the valley the two men parted, when the afternoon was well along. Step by step the one walked along, then began running, then jumped up and down with all his might to warm himself.

Unpityingly the cold winds swept by, requiring his utmost strength to battle against them. Nothing but snow, and ice and the bitter cold, not a raven to be seen.

"If I only had something warm inside me," murmured the man, "some soup, a sausage or two, anything—I could go to the end of the world. I must have something, if I beg for it."

A beautiful house appeared on the winter landscape, the house of Mr. Hartsee. This man formerly a small office-holder sat with his wife in a comfortably warmed room. They had married late in life when the habit of hoarding was well settled upon them, and together they watched, saved and hoarded, living in quietness and retirement the life of a pair of hamsters. No noise, no bustle, no confusion, each day like the one that had preceeded it.

Beside them in the living room lay an old fat dog and a lean cat occupied a cosy place near the kitchen stove on which a kettle of soup bubbled and steamed. Double windows kept out the wintry breezes; on the table stood a jug of new wine. A biting cold wind swept the evening clouds along over the snow covered expanses.

Mr. Hartsee looking out on the cheerless scene, remarked: "It's comfortable here, I'm quite suited to remain at home."

Just at this moment, the maid, a young girl, announced:

A Cheering Word.

"A poor journeyman is outside."

"You know very well, Theresa, that to every worthy beggar we give three pfennig, so why do you come to me with a beggar's tale?" said the mistress, angrily looking up from the paper which she was reading.

"He is very cold," ventured the maid and has a long distance to go," and her voice trembled. "He asks that we give him something to eat, and allow him to come in to warm himself, and I thought—"

"Theresa, you need think nothing," interrupted Mrs. Hartsee.

Mr. Hartsee said: "Go yourself, wife, and send the beggar off. Who knows what the dangerous man may have in mind with his tale of cold and hunger? I want order and repose, and I can't have strange men brought under my roof. Go, go, the door is standing open, and it is cold on my feet."

The wife rose and went slowly to the door, like a police magistrate, and found there the young journeyman.

"What are you doing in my kitchen?" said she sharply.

"I beg you to let me warm myself a little. It costs you nothing," said the man.

She took a ten pfennig piece, gave it to him and said:

"Here, that's enough for you. Begone. On principle we never let beggars into our house."

"I beg you, dear woman, for the sake of the good God, let me warm myself. If you do not wish to trust me in your kitchen let me come into your sitting-room."

"That would be better indeed!" replied the woman sarcastically.

"Go beg a dozen more pieces of money to put with that which you already have, and then warm yourself where you choose. There are inns enough. Begone, I say. I wish nothing more to do with you."

The journeyman laid the ten pfennig piece on a chest that stood near him, saying:

"Keep your money, Madam, then I will have nothing to thank you for."

This remark annoyed the old couple exceedingly and furnished a topic of conversation for the evening, but the story of suffering roused no sympathy in their hearts.

Out in the cold, the poor man said to himself:

"I'm weary of the struggle, but in God's

name, I take myself on my way again. I'll not kill myself until I get over the Roggenthal."

On and on he went, over the railroad embankment, and down into the valley, where there was less exposure to the wind. In Eybach lights shone from the inn-windows but he passed by.

"I beg no more to-night. That woman was too sharp with me."

Night was advancing and black against the sky stood the overhanging rocks and woods. Journeying on he prayed aloud and his voice was audible through the darkness of the night. He felt the death struggle upon him,

"I can go no farther. I must rest," said he, seating himself as he had done many times before. "In a few moments I will have gained strength enough, so that I can go up the mountain quickly and I'll be saved, — at home!"

He seated himself beside the road. The next morning a hunter passing that way saw something lying in the snow. It was the journeyman—frozen to death. He had fallen asleep, never to wake again, barely two hundred steps from his own door.

The Christ Child's Singer.

IN the old city of Beaucaire which lies on the bank of the rushing Rhone not far from the Mediterranean, and in the very heart of song-loving Provence, there stands a tiny house. Olive and mulberry trees grow in the garden that surrounds it and the noises of the city are there but faintly heard.

On Christmas Eve 1848, from the house chapel, in the upper story, a light glimmered and the villagers passing looked sadly toward the house for behind its walls was the son of a townsman whom all loved and honored, and for whose misfortune all grieved.

Eight years before this he had been ordained priest of God in the Cathedral of the city, and all the people with tears of joy saw the brilliant young man set out upon his life work, and congratulated his happy pious mother.

The celebrated chimes of the Cathedral, the great bell Bourdon, accompanied by many others, rang out in sweetest melody the joyful tidings, and friends and acquaintances whis-

The Christ Child's Singer. 103

pered, "The newly ordained priest will some day be Bishop." Who knew that this would not come to pass, for few worthier than he, have ever entered the priesthood?

On the eve before his ordination he wrote in a diary in which he placed an exact daily record of his life, these words: "O Lord, Thou who seest into the future, and into all secret things, if I am not to be a true servant at Thy altar, if I am some day to have the misfortune to bring disgrace upon the priesthood, let me die this night!"

On the day after his ordination these words were inscribed in the same book:

"Now I am a priest, a servant of Jesus Christ, Our Lord! Let me no longer give ear to the things of this world, let me only live for Thee Christ, for the souls of men. Impress deep in my heart the priestly virtues of humility, purity and love, and inspire me with greatest love of the cross and the Passion of Our Lord."

Blessed with shining gifts of spirituality, he was in his office of priest, as in his daily life, exemplary.

In his zeal for God's service, he thought too little of self and a sad thing happened. The long days of work and the longer nights of vigil, and the thousand mortifications of the flesh to which he subjected himself, told on his health, and finally a reaction came.

Standing in the pulpit uttering words, that, with irresistible eloquence, spoke his devotion to Our Lord, he suddenly stopped. His voice left him in the middle of a sentence, he cleared his throat and tried in vain to speak, but scarcely a whisper escaped his lips. Again and again he tried but to no purpose; his voice was really gone. Turning to the altar, with a look of resignation to God's will, he blessed himself and left the pulpit.

That was two years ago and since then the poor young priest has been unable to speak a word. Physicians have pronounced the case hopeless. He returned home to his mother and breaking all worldly ties, he lived with her a pious, silent, secluded life. As her love was the sunshine of his youth, so it was in his hour of trial. She it was who taught him to pray, to love God, to do good, to fear sin, and trained him in the ways of righteousness. In her he confided, finding comfort and sympathy in her every word and look.

With the Bishop's permission, the house chapel had been fitted up and here daily the priest and mother spent hours in prayer and contemplation; then the good God took the mother and the priest was left alone.

On this holy night, sad and lonely, he knelt before the manger, his heart bowed down by weight of sorrow. How gladly would he have gone forth preaching and teaching, but ill health added to his infirmity, kept him within doors. The candles burned low before the manger, the night wind howled and in his despondency Isaiah's prophecy, that on the coming of the Lord, the blind should see, the deaf hear, the dumb speak, came to mind. Suddenly the chapel became light. Who was it that entered, came to him, took him by the hand, led him to the altar and pointed to the manger?

He gazed and gazed for there were the Holy Family, the Christ Child sweetly sleeping in the manger, the Blessed Mother adoring, Joseph sitting by and the angel singing.

Listening he heard his mother praying, as she pointed to him.

"O Blessed Mary, to-day thou hast received the crown of motherhood, to-day thou hast learned the feelings of a mother's heart, O Mother of Christ, listen to the mother of the priest and give her child his voice."

The Blessed Mother nodded, saying by her look:

"Thy prayer shall be answered, but thy son must wait and must promise to use his voice in singing of Bethlehem, the birth of my Son and the Holy Christmas."

Tremblingly the priest questioned himself. Was he dreaming? Was it ecstasy?

Hark! the great bell Bourdon and the chimes of the Cathedral were ringing out over the city in sweetest harmonies, calling the faithful to join in their song, "Peace on earth, good-will to men."

The priest was consoled, and made a solemn vow worthily to sing the birth of Christ and its meaning to mankind. Hours of prayer and meditation made clearer to him, and presented in new beauties that greatest of all mysteries. He became, in truth, the singer of the Christ Child, the singer of Bethlehem and his songs are unspeakably beautiful, the music of angelic voices bringing to every soul the holy Christmas joys.

After ten years of silence during which time the poet-priest translated the music of angelic choruses into human verse, he regained his voice, and though in feeble health, took the parish of Gervasy, not far from Nîmes. Beloved by his people he brought them out of the state of indifference in which he found them, and through their generous offerings made of the tiny bare church a temple of beauty. Following the example of Our Lord they lived piously; their church fêtes were village fêtes as well, and their priest the pivot about which all moved.

Twice the Bishop offered him preferment; the first time he decided to remain in Gervasy because the people petitioned to have him, the second time because he himself begged the privilege of doing so

When the day was done and night had settled down over the earth, the priest worked. Song after song, in praise of the Christ Child, His wondrous birth, the Holy Night, the star of Bethlehem, the manger, the shepherds, poured forth from his pen.

Christmas in 1868, having grown weaker and feebler, in speaking of himself, he said:

"A year, perhaps two years more, then will my songs be ended," and he prayed:

"O God, let me die soon, that vanity may not lose for me the merit won by my labors."

In the following May when the flowers

bloomed and the birds sang, the priest of St. Gervasy was buried in the little church-yard and truly was he mourned, the sweet singer of Beaucaire.

NOTE. Ludwig Simeon Lambert, Curé de St. Gervasy, French poet, best known through his poem, "Bethlehem."

Saint Augustine's Convert.

A YOUNG girl stood weeping beside the coffin in which rested her mother, on the features of the dead the almost triumphant expression of tranquillity which marks those to whom the touch of death has seemed merely the finger of God.

Turning from the coffin with a sigh the daughter took a sealed packet from an old-fashioned chest which stood near by and gazing at the directions: "A keepsake for my dear daughter. To be opened after my death," kissed the words which the dear dead hand had penned.

Slowly she broke the seal. Inside the package were only some faded sheets of paper containing the simple and touching story of how the dead woman had learned to pray.

"I was a maiden of twenty when my father, a great manufacturer and merchant, took me on a trip to Switzerland. The summer weather was delightful and I was in a transport of enthusiasm and wonder over the beauties of nature in that enchanting land. I had not a care in the world. My health was perfect. I was the only child and heiress of a wealthy man. My mother died when I was a child, and I was the spoiled darling, the idol of my father, and yet many were the tender ministrations of a mother that I missed. Never had a mother's hand folded mine in prayer.

My first communion was merely a matter of course, accepted as a part of my education, with little sense of its divine and beautiful meaning.

I attended secular schools, was fashionably educated, mind and morals were carefully guarded, but things pertaining to God never entered my thoughts and many were the flippant remarks I made concerning church-going. I seldom attended church, as my father considered it unnecessary.

'Do your duty in the world, my child,' he often said, 'Be truthful, honest, gentle; further than that father or husband can always decide for a woman.'

I believed him without questioning and lived like a heathen. No crucifix hung at the head of my bed; no picture of the Blessed Mother decorated the walls of my room. I worked industriously and did not think of the future and eternity.

We spent a fortnight in Ragatz in the Swiss Mountains and I much enjoyed the lovely scenery in that pleasant spot.

One day we went on an excursion by rail to Coire, and accidentally, I was separated from my father. I waited for him at the station until it grew late, then decided to return to Ragatz by myself.

The train was full. I seated myself opposite a man whom I soon discovered was intoxicated. I drew down my veil and looked out of the window to avoid his impudent stare.

Much embarrassed, as the man became more and more bold, I rose to try to find another seat, when a courteous voice said:

'Pray take my seat, madam,' and I saw a Catholic priest beside me. He appeared to me like an angel from heaven. I thanked him with words and look and took his seat, where I was undisturbed for the rest of my journey.

The drunken man, however, was terribly enraged. He reviled priests and Jesuits, then cursed them violently and the men present laughed at his impertinence.

The priest made no reply to his remarks, but sat quietly looking out of the window, and at last we reached Ragatz. I rose to leave the train, as did the priest. I thanked him again for his kindness and expressed regret that he had subjected himself to such insults on my account.

Later we met at the hotel and he became a friend of my father, going with us on many excursions among the mountains. On our way to Pfäfers one day, I remarked that we had visited Regensburg, Nürnberg, Bamburg and Munich. He asked me if I went to the Bamburg Cathedral, and I remarked flippantly that I never went into churches as I did not like their atmosphere.

I shall never forget the expression of surprise that passed over the priest's face and the look of sorrow that he gave me.

A strange feeling came over me. I began to wonder why I was an object of disapproval to so good a man, and my heart was unquiet.

A few days after this he left Ragatz, after having exchanged a few calls with father and on parting I gave him, as a little token of remembrance, a costly vase filled with edelweiss, a vase which he could use upon the altar of his village church,

Saint Augustine's Convert.

He begged me to accept from him a small picture painted on a piece of parchment — the Crucifixion, the Saviour on the cross with outstretched arms, and underneath was written in large letters the words:

'O Lord, from Thee we came and our hearts are restless till we rest in Thee! St. Augustine.'

These words sank deep into my heart. I was possessed of a vague longing—I knew not for what. I began reviewing my life and found that it had been a very superficial one.

We traveled on to Bregenz, lingering long in the charming city by Lake Constance.

I often strolled about by myself as father found walking in the mountains tiresome. One afternoon fancy led me through the village and into the valley beyond the church, by the Convent of the Dominican Sisters, where, turning a corner and advancing a few steps, I found myself before a large door. Seized by a sudden and strange impulse I entered.

The Convent Chapel was quite empty and wonderful stillness reigned. Here with the world shut out, overcome by an unseen power, I felt myself translated into another realm.

All was so quiet, so beautiful, so unspeakably peaceful! At the sides of the altar were pictures, the Sorrowing Mother, the Saviour in priestly robes pointing to His Heart. I sat down and gazed spell-bound. In the choir-loft I heard sounds, light footsteps, then all was still. It was the Sisters who had come to Compline and I heard one faint voice chanting, then another and another until finally all the Sisters joined in a chant which rose heavenward, the virgin prayer of the nuns.

I did not see the nuns who were chanting but I listened with more wrapt attention than I had ever given to the most celebrated singer.

What sorcerer was it that made these voices so pure, so clear, so sweet, that they held one entranced? They seemed to be angel voices, and I listened until the last sound of the chant had died away. Then came a soft tone from the organ and the unseen choir began singing: Salve Regina.

I remembered a prayer that I once learned in school. As the words: 'Et Jesum benedictum fructum' rang out, a voice within me said, 'Pray, poor lonely child, pray'; then came the soft melodious, 'O clemens, O pia, O dulcis Virgo Maria!' and I could no longer control myself. I began to weep bitterly. I felt so wretched, so unspeakably unhappy that I wished to die. All joy seemed to have gone from my life, and I felt myself an outcast deserted by the world. My heart cried out against all that it had created for itself. I threw myself on my knees and cried aloud, my voice echoing in the still chapel.

'O Lord, from Thee we came and our hearts are restless till we rest in Thee!'

My whole soul, my very being went out to God; I asked pardon, forgiveness, belief, trust, grace, love. I know not what I said or how long I remained there. When I roused myself, my heart was light, and the way was clear to me. But what was I to do? How begin a life of devotion?

I found an old woman standing outside the chapel begging. I gave her some pennies and she said: 'Dear child, when you give alms, do not forget the nuns. They are poor, poor as I am. One can fairly see hunger in their eyes?'

This seemed a voice from God and I went to the door, rang the bell and gave my purse, filled with gold to the Sister who stood at the portal. She seemed much surprised and I said hesitatingly, as she took it:

'Will you pray for me, Sister?'

'O certainly, we will all together to-night begin for you a Novena.' Then she disappeared.

The prayer of the nuns finished what the look of the priest had begun with God's grace.

We stopped in Riedenburg for a month, and I received instructions from the priest who had been the means of my conversion, by giving me St. Augustine's words to fill my heart with unrest, the unrest only to be allayed by the divine hand which implanted it within my soul.

There I received communion and after that remained steadfast in the Lord. And now, dearest child, with God for witness, I declare to you the happiest hours of my life have been the hours spent alone with God in prayer and at communion.

I beseech you in these my last words to you, to learn to pray, and to pray in every moment of your life. No saying is truer than that of St. Augustine:

'O Lord, from Thee we came, and our hearts are restless till we rest in Thee!'"

CHRISTMAS IN THE SNOW.

ON the holy Christmas morning between the hours of three and four, a sleigh drawn by two powerful horses sped along through the woods, over a country road. Silent, as if sunken in deep slumber, lay the winter landscape beneath its mantling shroud of snow that bent low the branches and twigs of the trees of the forest and buried road and pathway.

The moon was full, the stars high up in the arch of heaven shone brightly, while those nearer the horizon were enveloped in clouds.

The two occupants of the sleigh spoke only now and then; the one sat on the high seat in front and drove, the other leaned comfortably back in the lower seat behind, and the snow from the horses' feet flew about them in a fine mist.

As the horses sped on, wood and hill and rock, silhouetted against the sky, disappeared behind the riders, and in the distance rose the outlines of the houses of a village with here and there a light, while the high narrow chapel windows sent out a bright glimmer.

A few moments and the sleigh was standing before the chapel.

The priest (for priest he was) and driver got out, shook off the snow and greeted the people standing about and then the mass began. The church was filled to overflowing. In awesome silence the people knelt, even those outside, trembling with cold, knelt in the snow, pulling their cloaks close about them.

Now and then, a glimpse through the open door, of the brilliantly lighted altar, the tiny manger containing a wax figure of the Christ Child, and the priest offering the sacrament, made them oblivious to snow and cold and wind. Then when the Sanctus rang, it told the good people at church, the sick and all those obliged to remain at home, that the Son of God was in their midst.

The first mass having ended, the people inside the church changed places with those outside. Among those passing out was Mr. M., a stalwart, robust man, the wealthy landowner, who dwelt in the castle on the hill beyond the village. He took a place apart from the people who looked wonderingly at him.

Christmas in the Snow. 119

For years he had been seen at church only at rare intervals, and not even at Easter time; therefore the people were surprised that he had come the long distance from his castle, to this early service, and that he would stand outside in the snow. With folded hands he held his cloak about him and seemed unmindful of the icy wind that blew hair and beard and mantle.

The people began telling their beads and in harmonic triad the prayer rang out, "And blessed is the fruit of thy womb, Jesus, whom thou, O Blessed Virgin, hast borne."

One could distinguish the soprano of the children, clear and high, the soft deep tones of the alto carried by the women, and the bass of the men, among whom Mr. M's voice was heard.

The second mass having ended and those inside having changed places with those outside, the third began. Mr. M. was urged by a neighbor to enter, but he said:

"Oh, no matter about me, friends. I'd rather stand out here. The mass will not last so very long," and so he stood for a second half hour in the cold and the snow, and during the Litany joined in the responses:

"Have mercy upon us."

The service ended, the priest came out, shook hands with his friends and chatted pleasantly.

An expression of surprise and pleasure passed over his face at sight of Mr. M. and he said to him:

"This is literally 'a white Christmas in the snow.'"

"Yes, yes, father," he replied, "and I hope the rest of the old saying, 'Easter, clover blooms will blow,' will come true."

"Merry Christmas to you Mr. M." cried the priest as he drove off.

* * *

During the last of Lent, the priest was walking slowly along a country road. Green fields stretched out on either side of him, and the song of birds, and the sunshine brightened the quiet spring landscape. He was thinking of a funeral, that of Mr. M., that he was to conduct on the morrow.

Mr. M. had died suddenly of a fever, after only a short illness.

Absorbed in thought the priest stopped and gazed absently at a field of clover when he was roused by the sound of a well-known voice, that of the assistant priest from the chapel, saying:

"Why so thoughtful, father?"

"I was thinking of Mr. M's answer to me Christmas morning when I said to him: 'A white Christmas in the snow,' and he quoted the rest of the old saying about 'clover blossoms for Easter.' Man little knows what the future may bring forth. Mr. M. so stalwart and robust, and in the prime of life, was not one that seemed destined for an untimely death, but to-morrow he will be buried under the clover."

"May he rest in peace," said the young priest fervently. "Mayhap on the Christmas morning in the cold and snow, his troubled, repentant soul, made its peace with God, God, who gives and God who takes."

Three Prayers.

"NOW you can see just how much we have to eat," said Arnold sullenly and morosely to his wife and sons, sturdy boys of seventeen and eighteen, as the family were gathering for the evening meal a few days before Christmas.

It was a gloomy household, for the three strong, able-bodied men were out of employment.

"None of you were dismissed from your positions," said the wife gently.

"No, not dismissed, but for a fortnight we have had no work and here are eight persons to feed, and we have hardly a piece of money in the house. The doctor, the apothecary, and the undertaker took the last of our savings at the time of grandmother's sickness and death."

"Do not scold, George," comforted the wife. "It is God's will. Be submissive. 'The Lord giveth and the Lord taketh away,' and surely He will not forsake those that minister to their parents with their last pfennig."

"But here are three of us out of work because the factory shut down. That could not be avoided, perhaps, but in another fortnight we will be starving, for the little we have will barely last two days, and in midwinter it is impossible to get work."

"It is not winter yet," said the wife cheerily. It is so mild that we need very little fire. Be glad that it is not cold; that is at least, something to us in our troubles."

"Yes, but there is no work and no profit," muttered George under his breathe.

"Do not fret father," said one of the boys, "the dear God does not desert those, who do not desert Him. I will go up and down the streets to-morrow begging for work."

"And I, too, father," cried a ten-year old girl. "And, I," "And I," "And I," came in chorus from three smaller maidens.

"God bless you my children, you are my comfort, my joy," said the father, "and the more there are of you, the dearer you are to me. Now pray that God will send your father work this day."

"Yes, father, we will," was the answer, and immediately they began loudly to pray:

"In the name of the Father, Son and Holy Ghost."

"How many Our Fathers shall we say, Papa?"

"Seven," replied the mother earnestly, "for the seven Dolors of Mary and five for the five wounds of Christ." The prayers of mother and children floated softly heavenward and the father and two sons knelt down with them.

This happened in a poor little street in one of the great capitals of Europe.

At this same time hunter Braff sat eating his evening meal, his eyes wandering anxiously to the bed in the adjoining room on which lay his young daughter. Pale and emaciated, with the expression of angelic purity and serenity that marks those to whom death is no stranger, she awaited the beckoning call of God.

"Papa, are the gentlemen going hunting to-morrow?" came softly from the lips of the sufferer.

"Yes, child, and unfortunately to-night I must go to prepare for their sport, then I must be up early to-morrow to direct the gentlemen where to find the game, and the hunt will last for three or four days."

"Oh, father, your being a poacher is the hardest of all for me. There are no men that—" she shuddered and did not finish.

"Cloudy, misty weather like this is unfavorable for shooting for it is hard to see game at a distance. However, it is so warm one can remain out-of-doors for a long time without suffering. Game is fat and plentiful and it will be wonderful if they do not get a great deal.

"O father, these men! I do not want you to go. I do not want to be alone."

"Hush, hush! be quiet, my child. During two or three days I'll have little rest, but I'll earn much gold."

"And the poor beasts out in the forest!" added the invalid. "I pity the poor does."

"And won't you think of me and pity me, Agnes?" sighed the father.

"O papa, yes, of course. But, do you know when you come back from the chase, I'll be in heaven, or in purgatory at least."

"My child, do not say such things," cried the father.

"No, dear, dear papa, I know surely that when I die you will be with me. It never takes long, that I've been told lots of times, and I feel that it is so. Can you not stay with me to-morrow?"

"My darling child, when gentlemen wish to go hunting the good Lord himself would hardly be able to prevent them. I must go."

Poacher Braff arose from the table, went to the bed of his daughter, smoothed her pillow, raised it a little higher, gave her his hand and said:

"As soon as I can, I will return and do not be frightened when you hear me. Good night, my Agnes!"

He went out and the maiden raised her thin hands toward the picture of the Blessed Virgin that hung near the bed and prayed:

"Remember me, O sweetest Virgin."

This happened in the south of Germany in a poacher's hut not far from a great wood.

Two boys knelt in a poor little chamber beside their bed and said their prayers while the moon, scarcely peeping out from behind the cloud, shone dimly through the roof-window. They prayed that their father might not be obliged to go to work on the day after the morrow because there was to be a Christmas entertainment and they were to sing and wished to have their father present.

The mother sat sewing and patching, weeping and praying between times that her husband might be able to go to mass on Christmas night. If he could only go to church in the forenoon of the day before Christmas she

Three Prayers.

would willingly give up the idea of his going on Holy Night.

Who was her husband?

A railroad conductor named Werner. Day or night he had little rest and was unable to go to church often. The loving wife prayed with her children that her husband might go with them to enjoy the Christmas festivities.

The husband was assigned extra work and sadly and disappointedly he said: "My fate is sealed for Christmas. I get extra duty."

This scene took place in the home of the railroad conductor Werner in a city in southern Germany.

* * *

The dear God looked down on his suppliant children on this evening, well pleased.

With His all-seeing glance He gazed upon the clouds moving restlessly above the earth and by that glance of love suddenly they were imbued with new life. The millions of water drops in them began to freeze and fell upon the earth in tiny snowflakes until it was covered with a thick mantle of white. The drizzling rain that had been coming down for so long within a half hour changed to snow. People at first scarcely noticed the change for the countless flakes melted in the mud and water, and silently the earth became whiter and whiter until the snow was master. The world slept and dreamed to awake to the beautiful scene.

At eight o'clock one of the sons of the factory-worker went out into the town and found at the nearest sign-post a notice, put up by the police authorities, saying: "Men wanted to remove snow from the streets. Pay, thirty pfennig per hour."

Within a half hour father and sons were at police headquarters and received employment, employment which lasted from eight to ten days, and brought them daily from seven to nine marks.

"Dear husband," said the wife, "do you not see that God has sent work to you from out the sky?"

Next morning early when poacher Braff went to meet the hunters it was very evident that hunting was impossible for the snow was a meter deep in places and great branches had broken and fallen to earth under their burden of snow.

The disappointed gentlemen returned home for not even a poacher could think of venturing out.

Three Prayers.

The poacher's daughter said:

"See, father, the dear God has taken the gun from the worthy as well as from the unworthy hunter. Now you can stay with me till I die."

Two days after this she died, and with a virginal wreath upon her white coffin was laid to rest under the snow.

Early that morning conductor Werner's train started out from the station but was compelled to return on account of the snow blockade, so the workmen were dismissed until afternoon. Mr. Werner went to church in the morning and as conditions were unaltered in the afternoon, he was able to attend the entertainment and heard his children sing as shepherd boys.

* * *

The great snow-fall was the answer to three prayers, and angels and saints joined in singing "Ice and snow praise the Lord in all eternity."

Ecce Homo.

IN the lovely little village of Boutiers nestled among the mountains of the Savoy Alps, there dwelt a young girl, Eugenie, more beautiful than any of the maidens of the town.

She was an only child, spoiled by her parents, beloved by her friends, and it is not surprising that at nineteen she considered herself, as others assured her she was, "the belle of the town."

She had so sweet a disposition, so engaging a manner, she went to church so often, prayed so devoutly that no one dreamed that her religion was but one of duty and outward observance, not one of the heart.

Love of admiration was her great fault. With her mirror she held long tête-á-têtes: she liked far better to see the lovely vision of girlhood which she beheld reflected into her smiling eyes, than to gaze upon the statues of the saints within the dim old village church.

Adoring friends kept telling her that a girl of her birth, beauty and education must look forward to some high destiny, and Eugenie believed herself called to a great mission.

So deceived was she, that she deemed herself humble and did not dream that to awaken her would take a vision as startling as that which awakened Saul of Tarsus and changed him into the holy St. Paul.

One evening in the year 1815, Eugenie was returning from a ball, where, with her parents, she had met with the élite of the land. Eugenie had been radiantly lovely in her white silk ball gown, with jewels gleaming in her hair and at her throat; and many had been the envious glances cast at her by the women and many the flattering remarks made to her by the men.

"Dear child," said her mother sweetly, "what joy you have given us this evening!"

And the father added:

"Next winter we will go to Paris. There our Eugenie will be in her proper sphere!"

The girl smiled well pleased as the carriage stopped at their door; they descended and entered the house. Eugenie bade her parents good-night and accompanied by her maid, retired to her boudoir.

"Truly a fairy princess!" exclaimed the maid, who had been with Eugenie since infancy and adored her young mistress.

"Indeed, I felt like Cinderella at the ball," answered Eugenie and she began telling all she had seen and heard during the evening, and how she alone had been the centre of attraction.

"Indeed, my beloved mistress, you are destined for something higher than remaining in this poor little village! You must go to Paris, to America, to Rome, where the noblest women in the world are to be found!"

Eugenie remained silent, but she could not conceal the pleasure that this flattery gave her.

"It is only the truth that I tell you," continued the maid. "Do you not believe that you were created for grand things? Do you consider that a man holding a civil office here, or a man in mercantile business would be a suitable person for you to link yourself with for life?"

"Oh!" cried Eugenie quickly, "Truly I have never yet as thought of marriage, but

Ecce Homo. 133

when, some day, I do choose a husband, he shall be the noblest and best in all the land."

At these words she rose erect and proud, and there was a sublimity in her eyes that commanded respect. It was plain to be seen, that, although she was vain, she had a horror of anything low and that the pure aspirations of a chaste soul filled her breast.

Eugenie still attired in full ball costume, went into her sleeping room and saying to her maid:

"You are tired, go and rest. I will undress myself; good night," crossed the room, casting but a careless glance at the crucifix beside her bed. At the back of the room stood a mirror reaching from the ceiling to the floor, that gave the young girl a full-length reflection of herself.

Tall, slender, beautiful she stood—a youthful figure clothed in a soft shimmering robe of white with bands of brilliants in her hair and about her neck, and bracelets upon her snowy arms.

Eugenie looked at herself admiringly. She was indeed beautiful. She raised her eyes heavenward, clasped her hands and whispered,

"Dear God, lead me to that high destiny for which I was created."

Had she realized that the prayer she offered up was not an expression of humility but of pride, she would not have dared to utter it so fervently, but scarcely thinking of aught save pleasure in her own beauty, she complacently again turned her eyes to the glass.

What change was there? She staggered back and almost fell. There, before her was the Christ, the Saviour, gazing upon her sadly.

Blood was flowing over His temples and cheeks, a crown of thorns encircled His brow and cruelly pierced the flesh; the holy face had sunk upon His breast; the lips moved painfully, there was unspeakable agony in the dark burning eyes which, though under the fearful thorns, looked compassionate and gentle.

With blood streaming from the wounds, the tall figure stood before her, clad not in splendor but in a blood-stained purple robe.

"Learn of me, for I am meek and lowly of heart," said a voice, whether aloud or whether only in her inmost soul, she knew not. She saw no one beside her and the appearance of the Christ lasted but for a moment.

"Dear Christ, forgive!" she cried as she fell upon her knees upon the floor.

Ecce Homo.

"Oh! of what sins, of what vanity, of what pride, I have been guilty! O, who art Thou, my Lord, and what am I in Thy sight?"

And, as if the ball dress that she wore, were itself a sin, rising she cast it off, pulled from her hair the comb and from her arms and neck the jewels and laid them aside.

Praying until the early dawn crept through the valley and the morning sun shone into her room, she saw the future clear before her.

She had come to the realization that of all things, Christian perfection is the highest, and she decided that the Son of God Himself should be her only bridegroom.

Her resolution was made and she never wavered from it.

* * *

It is now many years since all this happened and he, who writes this tale, stood one beautiful October afternoon before the entrance to the Convent *Trinita dei Monti* in Rome. The purple shades of the late afternoon were round about it, and bathed in gold, high over the sea of houses of the Eternal City, rose the dome of St. Peter's and the Vatican. When some moments later the door opened, he entered the Convent of the Sisters of the Sacred Heart and wandered about through the halls he stood in the place where Eugenie's life ended.

NOTE. Eugenie entered the convent of the Sacred Heart as a novice on St. Conrad's Day, 1816. In the year 1820, she was sent as missionary to St. Louis, and afterwards returning to Rome, was for years Mother Superior of the Convent, *Trinita dei Monti*, where she died in 1842.

www.ingramcontent.com/pod-product-compliance
Lightning Source LLC
Chambersburg PA
CBHW031324160426
43196CB00007B/658